FIREBRAND

FIREBRAND

DISPATCHES FROM THE FRONT LINES
OF THE MAGA REVOLUTION

CONGRESSMAN
MATT GAETZ

BOMBARDIER
B O O K S

A BOMBARDIER BOOKS BOOK
An Imprint of Post Hill Press
ISBN: 978-1-64293-764-0
ISBN (eBook): 978-1-64293-765-7

Firebrand:
Dispatches from the Front Lines of the MAGA Revolution
© 2020 by Congressman Matt Gaetz
All Rights Reserved

Cover photo by SG
Cover art by Cody Corcoran

Post Hill Press
New York • Nashville
posthillpress.com
Published in the United States of America

1 2 3 4 5 6 7 8 9 10

*This book is unapologetically dedicated
to my country—and the Firebrands everywhere
who love and protect her.*

CONTENTS

One	Sex and Money	1
Two	Lighting the Torch	17
Three	Russia Hoax	35
Four	A Perfect Call	57
Five	Enemy of the People	71
Six	Mar-a-Lago Magic	87
Seven	Two Parties, One Scam	95
Eight	Ending Endless Wars	101
Nine	China Is Not Our Friend	117
Ten	Sports Fan	131
Eleven	A Birthright Worth Defending	143
Twelve	Big Tech Hates America	157
Thirteen	Revenge Porn Chivalry	169
Fourteen	Uncanceled	177
Fifteen	Air Force One: Of Victories and Quarantines	191
Sixteen	A Green Real Deal	199
Acknowledgments		211

CHAPTER ONE

SEX AND MONEY

I DIDN'T SHOW UP TO SELL OUT. POLITICIANS ALMOST ALWAYS SAY the right things while campaigning. That's not hard if you're a halfway competent actor—and all politicians are actors.

Politics, they say, is show business for ugly people. The real question is who writes the scripts and produces the acts. You are governed by the theater geeks from high school, who went on to make it big booking guests on the talk shows. Ignore them and they'll ignore you, and you'll go nowhere fast. The hairdressers and makeup ladies and cameramen pick our presidents. As well they should. They are closer to the viewers and therefore the voters.

When Sen. Ted Cruz lost the 2016 Republican presidential nomination, he whined to his Black Gold backers that the media had given Donald Trump millions of dollars in free media exposure. You get "earned media" by *earning* it, Ted. And if they won't have you on, don't worry. Our generation doesn't flick channels for its MTV but will do anything for "the Gram." I grew up in the house Jim Carrey lived in in *The Truman Show*. I know that all the world's a stage, especially when we all have cameras with phones. Stagecraft *is* statecraft.

Speaker of the House Paul Ryan once knocked me for going on TV too much, without considering that maybe his own failures as a leader stemmed from spending too much time in think tanks instead of in the green rooms where guests wait to appear on TV, and are thereby connected to the dinnertime of real Americans. I take his recent elevation to the board of News Corp., the parent company of Fox News, to be his very silent apology.

It's impossible to get canceled if you're on every channel. Why raise money to advertise on the news channels when I can make the news? And if you aren't making news, you aren't governing.

The Justice Democrats take it a step further, recruiting candidates through casting calls that look more like Hollywood auditions than politics, screening applicants from a given district who sound good delivering their pre-scripted talking points and then backing them. Through this system of political performance art, the rising socialist Left found their female lead in Alexandria Ocasio-Cortez of New York, now perhaps the most powerful member of the House. FDR, JFK, LBJ, AOC: the Left memorializes its best with their initials, which its allies in Big Tech are happy to turn into trending hashtags while they shadowban those of us getting the real truth out.

President Trump knows talent when he sees it. He knows AOC has star power, which is why he so effectively trolls her fellow New York Democrat Chuck Schumer with the prospect of an AOC primary for his Senate seat. The president knows AOC and I are friendly, and on more than one occasion he has checked on my progress in encouraging her potential Senate run.

Once the good talkers get to Washington, they don't suddenly break bad. It's more that Washington presents them with a lot of distractions that make it, shall we say, easy to forget the principles they touted on the campaign trail. You don't drain the swamp; the swamp drains you. Of course, it's even easier to be distracted if you never had any principles. The emptiest of vessels become the most corruptible of officials.

D.C. distractions take two forms—sex and money. Getting paid and getting laid. Now, those aren't inherently bad things. In America, a bounty of both is to be honored and celebrated, not chastised. Congressmen shouldn't betray their country for them, though—yet too many do. In our time, all the politicians want to be celebrities while the celebrities want to be politicians. It's hard to party like a rock star when you're living on a public salary, so others pick up the tab—at a very steep price. It's just your soul—though no one really believes in that because it can't be monetized.

Washington, unfortunately, can be a very sexy city. Kissinger said power is the ultimate aphrodisiac, and D.C. covets it like the opioids the country can't seem to get enough of.

This town is full of celebrities making TV shows and movies, famous politicians, people gaining or losing power, scenic architecture, nubile coeds, embassy parties, and countless cosmopolitan fancies that stun those of us who show up as rural out-of-towners. It should both horrify and enlighten you that Bill Clinton said *House of Cards* wasn't far off the mark.

D.C. is said to have the highest concentrations of spies and hookers on the planet. It is often difficult to tell which is which, and that is by design. Influence peddlers are usually attractive or willing, or both. It helps them achieve their goals. So even if you don't think of D.C. as very tempting, you should stay on your toes here lest you get seduced for one purpose or another. A smiling face might not conceal a dagger, but it could hide someone's hope of getting a rider added to an agriculture spending bill. And if they can't seduce you, they'll get your spouse or your kids—just to get to you. Daniel Golden recounts in his book *The Price of Admission* that when Congress sought to regulate the multibillion-dollar endowments of the top universities by forcing them to pay out 5 percent of their funds, the way private foundations already do, a disproportionate number of the children of members of Congress suddenly got accepted to their first choice of college. Curiously, that reform legislation then went away.

Nassim Taleb says we like our heroes free and unencumbered. Now, I ain't no hero, but that's through no fault of my own. I arrived in D.C. as a single man after a couple of long-term relationships that didn't work out. I knew going in how many people had been brought down by sexual missteps in this town, so I set some rules to help me err on the safe(r) side. In Washington, safe sex means in part: no dating lobbyists, no dating your staff members, and I should have added no dating reporters, but I didn't at first. One former member, Blake Farenthold of Texas, amazingly violated the first two rules in one fell swoop by propositioning a staffer to have a threesome with him and a lobbyist, leading to his resignation in 2018.

I'm stunned by those who do things like pen love letters to staff, such as Rep. Pat Meehan, Republican of Pennsylvania, who was elected in 2010 and, like Farenthold, ended up resigning in 2018 after declaring a staff member his "soulmate." The amazing part is that Meehan was on the Ethics Committee. On paper, he sounded like a well-behaved family man, so why not? Meanwhile, if you're a single guy like me, some people in D.C. get suspicious immediately.

One young fellow member told me he's dating his scheduler. They're happy. Blissfully in love, he says. I told him, keep in mind she's no longer working for you—you're working for her, not the public you swore on oath to serve. She'll be hailed as a hero the moment she decides to call it off and publicly complain about it. I'm not preaching, just advising. It's risky to date in a town where there's potentially a thin line between love and blackmail, or at least love and bad PR.

But we've got a president now who doesn't care for puritanical grandstanding or moralistic preening. He is a lot more direct, even visceral, open, and realistic about his likes and dislikes, so overall, this is a good time to be a fun-loving politician instead of a stick-in-the-mud. I have an active social life, and it's probably easier in the era of Trump. We've had "perfect family man" presidents before, after all, and many of those men sold out our country, even if their wives were happy the whole time.

If politicians' family lives aren't what really matter to the voters, maybe that's a good thing. I'm a representative, not a monk. The days in which candidates presented themselves in the agora wearing spotless white robes are behind us. I represent the Florida Men—and Women—who elected me. I hope to represent them at their best, but I also represent them at their worst—and I beg their forgiveness when I am at mine.

Now to money.

Nobody is really from Washington, but everyone there quickly forgets where they came from. The question everyone asks aloud is, "Who do you work for?" The one they ask silently is, "And what can I get from you?" The answers are never: "The American people," and "Not a damn thing." The sociopaths who descend on Washington learn to substitute the will of the people (or political bosses) for their own, and they usually hope to make a buck in the process.

I arrived in D.C. with a duty to 700,000 constituents back in Florida. I seek to represent their interests, but the people who run D.C., the ones who stage-manage you around as soon you arrive, would prefer you forget your obligations at home and instead sit around, occasionally going to their cocktail parties and collecting PAC checks. The unstated assumption is that your votes will at least sometimes reflect their sources' pet causes when you aren't just rubber-stamping the party bosses' wants.

It's not as if legislators spend most of their time legislating, from what I can see anyway. They spend most of their time fundraising, getting buttered up by well-connected constituents or special interest groups, and looking for dirt they can weaponize against political opponents.

The party apparatus showed little interest in me before my primary, but when they decide you're already a winner—and will be able to bring more money into the party in the future—then they perk up. Once you're in the "in" crowd, Washington lets you know it. But it has a weird way of showing its enthusiasm.

As soon as I got to Washington, I was whisked to a restaurant with a fancy chandelier, where I found myself surrounded by congressional leaders, lobbyists, and newly elected legislators. Carafes of wine danced around the tables like ladies in beautiful red dresses, the steaks probably cost more than my kidneys would fetch on the black market, and there were all the artistic desserts you could desire—impressive to a North Floridian whose idea of "fancy dining" had long been fish that gets grilled but not put on a bun.

Addressing the crowd was then speaker Paul Ryan, since retired, a man who in the mid-2010s went suddenly from an admired symbol of the free market movement to the deeply unpopular symbol of the Washington establishment. But at this gathering in 2016, Ryan was still a kingmaker, if not a king, and the assembled lobbyists were his court.

It was the first time I had ever met him, and the first thing I saw him do on that occasion was to introduce an odd group of people he described as the individuals he considered really responsible for getting us newcomers elected: an array of lobbyists. Now, he never said we had to obey these lobbyists, nor was anything quite that crass implied. Rather, his behavior was a case of congressional leadership fulfilling its obligation to demonstrate to the lobbyists that leadership could provide *access* to the newly elected members. Unfortunately, for those inclined to compromise principles or seek handouts, access is half the battle.

The people who have a legislator's ear or who agree to give him donations don't necessarily pull the strings, but they garner more attention—"face time" in the parlance. They make deals, forge alliances, and their pet issues get remembered, unless the booze makes everyone forget last night's conversation, which is a very real occupational hazard in Washington. Those who attend these intimate gatherings get just a little more consideration than you do.

Even before the general election, those of us likely to be in the freshman class in Congress were told what the party's legislative agenda would be—as my predecessor, effective eight-term Congressman and Southern gentleman Jeff Miller, had told me would happen. As he also told me, one of the first suggestions we got from the party was the strong hint we should donate to other candidates, even if donating this late in the race might make little practical difference. It was a show of mutual support. We would be beholden to each other, and to the party, in ways difficult to forget or ignore later on.

Donations to the party do not officially determine which committees you'll sit on or how prestigious your spot will be, but unofficially money sure seems to make a difference. I won't pretend I walked away from the game. On the contrary, I was playing to win, and I did. I was eager to meet with Leader McCarthy in hopes of getting a spot on the Armed Services Committee, which is very important to decisions that affect the lives of many military personnel and veterans in Florida's First District. I expected that when I did meet with him, I'd have to explain the potential impact on my constituents, my relevant experience with military issues, and the ways in which I was (or was not) in sync with the rest of the party on military and foreign policy issues.

To my shock, he looked me straight in the eye and said it would be helpful if in the next ten days I could direct $75,000 "across the street," which meant into the coffers of the National Republican Congressional Committee. I frankly told my supporters back home about how things apparently work in D.C., and they agreed I should try rolling the dice. I quickly ponied up $150,000, twice the ask, and ended up not only on Armed Services but the Judiciary Committee as well. They even asked if I wanted anything else. If you "moneyball" it out, it sure makes sense for an ambitious member to participate in the system, whether or not he likes the system as a whole. But there is a difference between being of the system and playing the system.

Once given, they'll rarely take away your committee assignment, unless they really think you're a troublemaker. I hope mine aren't revoked when this book is published!

The big annual March dinner becomes a first assessment of how much you, the new member of Congress, owe the party bosses. Fortunately, since I had donated that $150,000 on the way into office, the party assessed my likely future contributions at $490,000, which is what the parties call your "leadership potential" in coded D.C. parlance, just as in Congress "compromise legislation" and "stakeholder consensus" are often code for "special interests teaming up across the aisle to screw Americans." I did bring in the expected amount that first term, but I'm unlikely to meet their expectations again, for reasons I'll explain at the end of this chapter.

Once you're in a position of prominence and power, there are always parties you can attend where you'll rub elbows with movers and shakers from various industries and pressure groups. But I don't know that I'd call those parties *themselves* much of a temptation for me. They're no "reward" or "pot of gold" I'm looking for, not some big pleasure-orgy—more like a very awkward and phony speed-dating session. For many people, though, events where they can meet the money-givers and other power brokers are the alpha and omega of the whole D.C. experience. Tedious and boring for most people, these events become the great aspiration for certain Washingtonians. Some people really do sell out through their stomach and liver.

Arizona's Rep. Andy Biggs, a great guy and chair of the House Freedom Caucus, does not have my anti-PAC rule but has his own balanced way of avoiding too much interaction with some of the people who surround them. He hosts his PAC fundraisers as concerts by his Mormon family band, in which he and some of his relatives sing, so you can attend those performances and not even talk to him. The donor types show up, pay, and leave. Hats off to him for making this excruciating process something where he doesn't have to be too phony face to face. What Andy lacks in tone and pitch he more than makes up for in volume and enthusiasm.

As for me, I'd rather be reading, talking to my constituents, or going on a date with someone who sincerely cares than dining with some of the money/power people, but members who reject that scene completely won't ascend the ranks of power. Committees are rated A, B, and C based in part on how much fundraising you have to do to get assigned to them. Freshmen are virtually never assigned to an A committee right off the bat. And you're liable to end up on a B or C permanently if you aren't up for playing the game.

What is likely more corrupting than all the literal money sloshing around, though, is the array of "lifestyle enhancements" available to those who hang around with the lobbyists and industry people: Super Bowl tickets, hunting trips, research junkets to glamorous locations, the sorts of things that can stealthily turn what is officially a $10,000 donation into something more like $100,000, all technically within the rules and in accordance with various limits on amounts and timespans-per-donation, and so forth. "Sure, the job only pays $172,000," Congressman-turned-lobbyist Jack Kingston told me on a flight from D.C. to Atlanta during my first year. "But with all the travel and fundraisers you get to do, it's more like a $400,000–$500,000 package. Take advantage of it!"

I should add that I don't think outlawing this kind of activity and replacing it with public (that is, government) financing of political campaigns would be a good solution. The government would end up pulling the candidates' strings, whereas the best political campaigns, the most sincere ones, are the ones funded by private citizens far from Washington, real grassroots outsiders. There are campaigns, especially for newcomers to Congress, funded by small communities, members of Boy Scout troops, baseball leagues, and so forth.

Sustainable, passionate movements of any kind always have private individuals willing to invest in them, and that should continue. The tragedy is that the big corporate donors have enough sway to make the whole process more like prostitution, or as if both parties are competing for boring gigs as valets. I used to think my party, the Republican Party, was at least a valet for *better* special interests than the Democrats', but I no longer think it makes much difference. The same entrenched interests give money to both sides.

The rising stars of the influence-peddling game are Big Tech, who don't seem to get sued or regulated a hundredth as much as you'd expect to see in any other industry that does some of the creepy things Tech does. They warrant their own chapter below.

President Trump represents a real change in some of these patterns, though. He may be rich, but he's also a perfect example of someone whose campaign thrived on small donations and the passion of individual voters. Trump is a geyser of small-dollar contributions. You don't produce rallies like his by hosting a couple of stiff corporate luncheons. That man is a real movement, and he's movement in the right direction, away from some of the undemocratic ills I've described.

Sure, money talks, but talking talks too. But you have to have something to say. And it's depressing how few do. President Trump knows that raising a ruckus raises your profile but can also raise an army of patriots. Message, movement, money, mobilization. In that order. He knows that is how you build a brand. Brands need slogans that feel real because they *are* real. "Yes, we can" gave us "Make America Great Again," both delightfully vague and subject to interpretation. Just who is the "yes" directed to? We "can do" what? To whom? Who is doing the making? What is great? And why again? Isn't America always great? Like an inkblot, Americans project their private hopes onto these slogans and make them their own in their own individual way. The moms and grandmas who were hand-sewing masks for loved ones during the coronavirus were making America great again. So too were the patriots who donated to the We Build the Wall crowdfunding campaign.

While President Trump pledged to build the wall, Bill Clinton promised to "build a bridge to the next millennium." (He neglected to mention that the Chinese and millions of illegal aliens were already coming across it.) I have my own infrastructure-themed slogan—#OpenGaetz—that comes from my days as an attorney, suing governments to open records for public review. Every gate needs a sentry, keeping a watchful eye on who comes and goes. Openness means honesty and awareness, not exhibitionism or naivete.

IT'S IMPORTANT, IF YOU'RE AN UNPRETENTIOUS, PSYCHOLOGI-
cally normal person, not to let yourself think Washington is full of
people who want to be your friend—or even want to debate policy
ideas with you.

Rep. Cathy McMorris Rodgers was the chair of the House
Republican Caucus when I arrived, and she surprised me by
calling me up and inviting me to dinner. I was honored! I thought
the dinner was going to be something small, but there were fifty
donors and lobbyists there—which was supposed to be the attraction, I now realize. At the door, the hosts handed out name tags, so
the donors could spot us and chat up the legislator of their choice.

I am seated at a table that doesn't even have Rep. McMorris
Rodgers at it, but, what do you know, her speech to the crowd
refers to me as her special guest, and she points me out to the
crowd as if I'm supposed to be grateful that they can all now flock
to me and I can harvest cash from them. I now understand why
many frosh in Congress are truly grateful to be pimped out like
this! And if they rake in a lot of donations, one way or another
they're supposed to bounce it right back to party leadership.

It's not just the Republicans, of course, and it's not just Washington. There are so many layers of lobbying that private companies hire lobbyists to pressure state legislators to take messages to
that state's delegation in D.C., as an indirect way to get Congress
to do what the companies want.

In other words, in America today, the lobbyists now lobby other
lobbyists, and so on up the chain, without the voters weighing in at
any point along the line.

Irrespective of which party is in power, then, the real winner in
Congress is often the special interest that shuttles the most money
to political campaigns. Committee assignments and leadership
opportunities are doled out to members *most* indebted to special
interests, not true leaders. Congressional staffers even use the

orientation process to tell new members exactly which PACs and special interests will donate based on which committee assignments you get and how much influence you'll wield.

Not everything PACs want is bad. Sometimes they're trying to get rid of the same regulations that annoy me. But the PACs don't exist to do good. That's incidental, if it happens at all. They exist to give big business what it most seeks—power over politicians to put their interests over America's. If that means ending a regulation, great. If it means creating one, so be it. Lower taxes? Raise taxes? Grant an exception? Whatever pleases the donors.

I should know. I've catfished hundreds of thousands of dollars from special interests. I never quite met their expectations, but I always knew what they wanted. And one thing federal PACs don't want is you looking behind the curtain at their corruption. They are fine with your chanting "drain the swamp" and denouncing D.C., but then they want you to do nothing as they make a few cosmetic adjustments that don't drain the swamp but turn it into their personal mud bath.

If petty distractions and temptations are the problem, it helps to take a step back and remember how much more enticing the original idea of America was. It's still inspiring. Our Founding Fathers did not commit treason against the Crown of England only for our generation to turn around and prostitute ourselves to globalist corporate interests. Our Founding Fathers pledged their lives, their fortunes, and their sacred honor to the cause of liberty. They wouldn't have accomplished much if a couple of steak dinners had been all it took to steer them off course. We still hear a lot about "fortune" in Washington, at least in the material sense. It's harder to find honor or sanctity.

The PAC donation process—with its expectations of exchanging favors for money—renders public service, which should be among our most noble vocations, dangerously close to the oldest profession. I've never turned tricks for Washington PACs, but I'm done picking up their money from the nightstand. That's why, as of 2020, I will never again accept a donation from a federal political action committee. Not one red cent. The American people are my only special interest.

I don't want to alienate my party, and I still greatly prefer the Republicans to the Democrats. But I'm the only Republican returning to Congress to make this "NoPAC" pledge. I'm joined in this pledge by California Democrat Rep. Ro Khanna.

Now, many other Democrats morally preen and posture for swearing off *corporate* PAC money—but they still gorge on union PACs, ideological PACs, and something ironically called "leadership PACs," which are mostly PACs for letting politicians and former politicians donate to each other. Talk about insider money!

Real leadership is telling people the truth. The truth is not that one party is out to get you and the other one is coming to your rescue. The truth is that Washington is partying on your dime— and the parties aren't even that much fun. Their ultimate purpose is to connect the real special guests (corporate lobbyists and the like) to the vast pool of taxpayer dollars, with the campaign money and party dues of us politicians as a mere admission fee— and any resulting government projects (including changes in law or regulation), if something actually gets done, as the evening's entertainment.

It's not a great way to govern. It's not even the most direct way to have a good time. It is terribly distracting, though, and even if you have no firm political philosophy, you would do well to treasure those few politicians who are adept at ignoring it all. Some people really enjoy it, and those are the ones you need to be worried about, whether they style themselves as right-wingers, left-wingers, or—sometimes worst of all—moderates.

As for me, I suspect I'm not going to be a lifer here. I've never missed the distractions of D.C. when in my beloved home state. Every day I spend in Washington, I miss the easy smiles, warm sands, shimmering emerald waters, and friendly greetings of my true home. I'll get done what work I can for the American people and my constituents back in Florida, and then at some point, I expect I'll get the hell out of here.

Meanwhile, like President Trump, I'm happy to fight the good fight—especially at a time when it can make a real difference.

CHAPTER TWO

LIGHTING THE TORCH

HOLT IS HOME TO FIVE HUNDRED OF MY CONSTITUENTS ALONG Interstate 10 in Northwest Florida. They farm, hunt, wear overalls, and love the USA, which more than a few of them have fought for. They wear blue collars if they wear collars at all. Their Ford pickups are covered in red mud and sport colors that never run or fade.

The center of commercial activity in Holt is the Stuckey's filling station, where my blue Jeep idled in the parking lot. I had pulled off the interstate to secure a good signal as I awaited the voice of the most powerful man in the world.

"Congressman Gaetz, this is the White House operator. Please hold for the president."

I love President Trump. I may never love another president. But this call worried me. For the first time, I had disagreed with the president publicly, on television. He doesn't love that.

Earlier in the day, the president went on record regarding special counsel Robert Mueller. He said he thought Mueller would treat him "fairly," which, of course, Mueller and his associates did not. Wishful thinking, Mr. President.

How to react to Mueller's appointment was the subject of much debate in the Republican conference at the time. The then speaker Paul Ryan and GOP icon Rep. Trey Gowdy surmised that Mueller was an unquestionable, unimpeachable hero. The thinking went: we should all praise Mueller, confirm the legitimacy of his team's investigative work, and pray that Trump hadn't done anything criminal. Besides, they thought, a President Pence—one of Congress's own—wouldn't be so bad. What couldn't be done at the ballot box could be done in the witness box.

Everybody looks for a scapegoat to excuse their own misdeeds. They didn't find any witches on this witch hunt, but they were prepared to drown Donald Trump and members of his family all the same. The president was innocent, but that was precisely the point. The process was the punishment—both for the president and for the people who voted for him. The deep state would run out the clock on this presidency. No "Make America Great" for you!

The Mueller probe was fake from the start. I said it then. We all know it now. My constituents saw Mueller for the fraud he was. They were right, and I was on the attack, tarred by the mainstream media as Congress's leading Mueller critic. What was meant as an insult then, I wear today as a badge of honor. To watch Mueller testify is to know he wasn't up to the job.

"A lone voice in the wilderness," my hometown *Pensacola News Journal* called me as I criticized Mueller and the entire notion of his appointment. Things weren't made easier by the president himself saying he would be treated "fairly" by the until then beloved Republican war hero.

When I was confronted on live TV with the president's praise of Mueller, I answered frankly. The president was mistaken, I said. This investigation should be stopped. It was an attack on the vote and voters, whether Trump believed that to be the case or not.

"Matt…it's your favorite president," I heard.

"Reagan?" I joked. President Trump was not amused. He moved on.

"I just saw you on television. I love the red tie. Keep doing what you are doing. Keep saying what you are saying. Don't worry about what I said today. That was for the media. I need warriors, you know what I mean?"

I knew exactly what he meant. Though President Trump longed to be free to realize his vision of restoring our nation to greatness, the beginning of the Trump era required a "warrior class" in Congress to step up and fight like hell for him, as he fought like hell for America. To be an effective fighter you need not wear the uniform—though some have, like Florida Governor Ron DeSantis—but you must be a fast thinker. And too few Republicans know how to think, let alone fight.

Our first one-on-one discussion lasted only twelve minutes, but there would be many more calls after that. The president has called me when I was in my car, asleep in the middle of the night on my Longworth Office cot, on the throne, on airplanes, in night-clubs, and even in the throes of passion (yes, I answered). Not to mention Christmas Day. Often but not exclusively at night. The president keeps odd hours. Now, so do I.

He has called me elated, tired, cursing, curious, screaming, and once when I was saying farewell to one of my constituents at Arlington. He swears at me with the enthusiasm of a New York construction worker, but he has also told me that he loves me. He has called to talk sports and to give me advice on my romantic misadventures. He's called when there were other people in the room and asked me my opinion of them while on the speakerphone.

It isn't who is seated with the president who shapes the world. It's those who listen to him and who he listens to on these late-night/early-morning calls. And given what I've learned about espionage in Washington from our government and others, I doubt we were the only ones on the line.

President Trump and I have an understanding and a newfound relationship that has only grown stronger with time. He can count on me to make arguments on the front line of the fight.

I hadn't finished my first year in Congress, but as I pulled out of the Stuckey's parking lot, I knew I had a closer relationship with the president than many who had served decades and held what Washington considered "real power" due to their titles and trappings.

But it didn't start that way. In fact, on the president's first day, I felt like little more than a distant observer.

You know your place in Washington when they put you in the nosebleeds. You seldom get handed a front-row seat to anything in life—not even if you're a newly elected congressman. In America's capital city, where they seat you reveals where they think you really stand.

At Donald Trump's inauguration ceremony I felt more like a movie extra than a leading voice in a powerful political movement. To the shock of many, Trump had faced down and defeated virtually every major institution in America: the Democrats, the media, senior leadership of the intelligence community, the bureaucrats, and even plenty of Republicans.

In fact, many of the establishment Republican congressmen, donors, and other heralded figures who were to varying degrees anti-Trump in their hearts and minds (if not their words) had taken the same seats they would have occupied had we been inaugurating Jeb Bush, John Kasich, or Nikki Haley. Proximity to power is something the establishment understands all too well. They were fine trash-talking candidate Trump on secret conference calls but now quickly scrubbed their #NeverTrump tweets.

From inauguration seats to senior administration positions to statements of administration policy, the establishment that loathes Trump relentlessly endeavors to stay close to him. They're established for a reason, and they're good at staying that way.

"Fight Washington, Restore America." This was the slogan that sent me to Congress after six years in the Florida Legislature. Serving in the Florida House of Representatives had been the public service honor of my life. During the 2010 Tea Party jolt of political energy, my community had placed trust in me as a twenty-six-year-old candidate among a field of five. I felt obligated to validate their decision by working hard and delivering results.

I ended my tenure in the state House as the powerful chairman of the Finance and Tax Committee after having also served as chairman of the Criminal Justice Committee. The priorities of my district were always reflected in the state budget. I took care of my people and they took care of me. This is the responsibility of leadership.

The first poll testing the viability of a congressional campaign following the unexpected announcement that my predecessor would retire had me down fourteen points to an older, better-known state senator. I'd end up beating him by fourteen, the rest of the field by more.

As the *Pensacola News Journal's* Andy Marlette would observe following one of the 2016 debates that sent me to Congress:

> *As far as sheer debate talent and readiness, nobody is close to Gaetz. That's not an endorsement or a criticism of other candidates. But as the saying goes, the guy just has mad skills. I don't know if he's more Steph Curry or LeBron James, but he's that good when it comes to rhetorical game time. He even inspired Sen. Evers to refer to him as a "slick-tongued lawyer" at one point. Gaetz seems to have the rare ability*

*to speak almost as quickly as he can think, which would
get most folks in deep, deep trouble. But whether you agree
with his politics or not, watching Gaetz on the debate stage,
you've got to admit that the guy is playing ball at a higher
level than most.*

Firebrands win elections. I've never lost.

Now that voters had given Republicans what we had always
asked for—unified control of the government—I was there to
capitalize on Trump's victory and shake things up. But I couldn't
fight for anyone from the rafters. I couldn't even hear. I would need
to fight for a better seat before restoring anything.

Little did we know at the time that the battle for the presidency was already underway and it called for the best brawlers
we had.

To the charge that I'm a young man in a hurry, I plead
guilty. But, thank God, America's oldest and greatest president is
young at heart. He expects you to have sharp elbows if you want
to secure a seat at his table. Earn your spot and fight to keep it, or
you're fired! And no, you won't be invited back next season. "I'm
not here to make friends," every reality TV star tells us. Neither
was I. I had a job to do.

Not that I—or Donald Trump—had a Rolodex full of Beltway
friends when we both traded the Florida swamp for D.C. And just
like the gators in Florida, some of these slithering swamp creatures
had seemingly spent millennia adapting to the sludge, only to face
what now threatened to be an extinction-level event.

It's easy to enjoy that moment when those who had taken shots
at candidate Trump during the campaign had to swallow the fact
that he was president. They likely fretted that #NeverTrump would
turn to #NeverHired—or #SoonFired by their constituents. With

millions of voters behind him, Trump's ratings were huuuuge. You dared not turn off your phone lest you missed his tweeting, which seemed equal parts executive order and savage taunt.

It has become fashionable to say that you wish the president would stop tweeting, but tweeting is communicating and communicating is governing. Had Donald Trump found a way to short-circuit politics, the way he seemed to short-circuit the politicians?

By his nature, Trump is a disrupter and a rebel. Yet even the most disruptive political leader faces huge, almost immovable obstacles in Washington, D.C. The Trump Train can get derailed despite its conductor's best efforts.

In fact, the Washington establishment had already decided how it would thwart our little revolution. Even before his inauguration, the Democrats leaked intelligence about the Trump campaign's purported ties to Russia. Rep. Maxine Waters had suggested that the 2016 election process was so tainted by Russian interference that we must deny the certification of the electoral college decision. The establishment, which for months had claimed that Trump had dangerous authoritarian impulses, turned out to be quite ready to declare the election null and void.

Trump's message was threatening precisely because it was so popular. The real danger in the minds of the Democrats and their mainstream media allies wasn't hackers from Russia but Trump's message to America: the idea that we could create a new conception of the public good based on sound money, strong borders, national pride, and respect for values founded in faith and tradition. No more big-shot politicians and corporatists wheelin' and dealin'!

Nor would the Democrats argue their side. Their strategy wasn't going to involve policy debates about Obamacare, the tax code, and so forth but an attempt to undermine the messenger.

Trump is an illegitimate president, they claimed, and he did not lawfully hold the office. Perhaps after watching Trump feed fifteen Republican primary opponents into the political woodchipper, the radical Left chose personal destruction over policy. The way to defeat Trump, they concluded, was to be as crass and hyperbolic as they mistakenly judged him to be.

After countless elections involving voting by the dead, bogus "October surprise" revelations, or coordination with transnational corporations and foreign political movements, this particular election was not up to the establishment's standards and had to be immediately overturned. The precise reasons would keep morphing over the next three years, as one invented argument after another crashed against the rocks of reality.

If they could get away with nullifying Trump's election, though, who's really in charge in Washington, D.C.? Might it be those same powerful figures seated so prominently at the inaugural that day? Is the deep state actually quite near and in plain sight? I wonder how many were thinking, "We'll tolerate this interloper and the populists who arrived with him—for now. Those we can't coopt we can undermine and ultimately destroy."

Almost as soon as we stepped off the inaugural stage, many powerful Washingtonians—including some Republicans and nonpartisan professional bureaucrats—would sign on to the anti-Trump bandwagon. They were quite accustomed to "waiting out" a shift in the political winds. Washington is full of "apolitical" professionals who are convinced that democracy is a formality and that true patriotism lies in maintaining their power as wise stewards of the political apparatus so that they can go on making decisions for the rest of us.

Republicans and Democrats, while bickering for show, had long since joined forces to *invade everywhere* militarily, *invite everyone* to immigrate, and *impoverish Anytown, USA,* by forging complicated insider trade deals that drain our economy and leave our towns and our families impoverished while enriching multi-national companies.

Worrying about these issues isn't quite the old, staid Republican agenda. But then, that agenda had been shaped by some of the very players arrayed that day on the National Lawn. They aren't monsters (mostly). But their interests have sharply diverged from those of the hundreds of millions of Americans they represent.

A course correction is urgently needed. An elite that ceases to think well of the people who grant it power deserves to be displaced. To conserve our way of life, we need to think radically about how to meet our obligations to our country. Every slogan of yesteryear, every program from once upon a time, ought to be retested to see if it still works. A new generation requires new thought from new leaders. The price of liberty is eternal vigilance—and careful, deliberate thought.

But from whom shall we get it? Our think tanks are running on empty. Our economic policy is stuck in the 1980s, our foreign policy in the 1950s, our social policy in the 1960s. Republican voters confronted with uninspiring agendas rejected low-energy "reform." They elected not a cautious caretaker but a brash, outspoken Firebrand.

Indeed, there's an obvious problem with the very idea of conservatism. For as long as conservatism has been a self-identified philosophy, about 250 years, its advocates have struggled with this conundrum: If your goal is to preserve a culture and a way of life, how do you ever make the case for changing it when radical reform is necessary?

There have been attempts to square this circle. Figures such as the late Sen. John McCain, very much the military man, have emphasized the get-tough "reform conservative" idea that when America recognizes problems, we just have to summon the will to

solve them, usually without considering the economic costs and
benefits or looking too closely at the leaders and institutions that
got us into the mess in the first place. Reform, like the British
ideal of the "stiff upper lip," becomes an exercise in stoicism, or so
we are told. We knew our duty, and we strayed a bit off course, but
if we stick to our guns, we'll see it through.

This philosophy isn't very American. It is certainly not the
philosophy of young Americans today. If something is broken, it
is our duty to fix it. Preferably yesterday. What the hell is taking
so long?!

Some rising voices in today's Republican Party, such as
Texas Rep. Dan Crenshaw, call that kind of resolve "fortitude."
I don't mean to dismiss this character trait. Who doesn't want
to be tougher? And where better to draw inspiration than from
those who have shown themselves willing to risk all and sacrifice
in battle? Yet the substitution of fortitude for imagination—our
capacity for seeing, feeling, touching, tasting with the soul—all but
guarantees failure.

If we emphasize the virtue of fortitude, failures of policy start
being seen as failures of the will, not the mind. It's not that we have
wrong or outdated ideas, we just haven't willed them to success.
Don't think too hard about the details, let alone challenge our own
longstanding habits and assumptions. We just have to summon up
that deep determination from inside us, don't you know.

The problem with romanticizing grit as a cure for what ails us
is that it all too easily becomes passive acceptance of a lackluster
status quo. At its worst, this kind of conservatism devolves into an
angry defense of the worst parts of how things are and the insis-
tence that questioning any aspect of the way America currently
functions is tantamount to treason. Fortitude too often asks people
to stare into a mirror and pretend it is a window to the future.

Americans are a hurried, impatient people. We don't have time to wait. Not at the DMV, and certainly not for the economy to rebound after a recession or a devastating pandemic. Manifest Destiny, dammit! We settle the West, we take Berlin, we jealously guard our rights. We even put people on the Moon because we can inspire through achievement. Justice delayed is justice denied, after all.

The best things about America didn't happen because we resolved to sit quietly and accept with stoic fortitude whatever fate doled out to us. That was the peasant life the first Western settlers abandoned to stand up and become a nation of greatness through ambition. We're the people of "Let's roll," "Give me liberty or give me death," and the "shot heard round the world." We don't defer to our leaders; we lead, they follow. "Make America Great Again" means we have to do the making in the here and now. No time to waste!

We sure didn't become the great nation we are by resolving to let Washington do whatever it likes to us so long as it makes the occasional feeble effort at "reform." And neither Donald Trump nor I was elected in 2016 to wait politely for Washington to improve itself. A slow path to reform is a path to degeneracy. Didn't we learn anything from Democratic politician Rahm Emanuel? A crisis is a terrible thing to waste, he said. And waste them we do, preferring to paper them over with more spending and more debt—more, more, more to get less, less, less done. We will always careen from crisis to crisis until we meet our challenges head-on, as President Trump does.

Stoicism is not statecraft. Calmness is not virtue. Millennials know that playing by the rules is a very quick way to lose the game. They saw their parents buy houses only to suffer foreclosures. They saw no-fault divorce shatter their families. They got college degrees only to be burdened by debt they can never pay off in a market that increasingly values cheap foreign labor and corporate bottom lines over jobs for hardworking Americans.

Indoor voices get indoor results. John McCain was beloved by the media that hates Donald Trump. There's a reason. He was running political plays from a losing playbook. He treated politics as though it were a country club where genteel men and women get together and negotiate the unconditional surrender of your rights, your job, and your voice. Even when we agreed with John McCain, he wasn't effective—and perhaps to his Democrat admirers that was the point all along. Playing by the quiet, reserved rules of the nightly news anchors, of Jeb Bush and his relatives, of coolly detached international diplomats, isn't governing; it's stifling that very real and urgent impulse to get mad, get organized, and win. Yes, "Build that wall!" Yes, "Lock her up!" We don't have time to wait politely while CNN's Chris Cuomo interrupts us.

We should be outraged sometimes. We should be animated, showing our disgust with a system that keeps forgetting we're here. We used to tar and feather tax collectors. Our Founders taught us that resistance to tyranny is obedience to God. We need more attitude, less fortitude.

Stoic fortitude without accompanying attitude is tantamount to accepting the way Washington already does things. You thought you stood firm, but the next thing you know you realize you're standing motionless while the system buries you alive, having tricked you into thinking you're "doing your duty" and "respecting the process" when you should have been raising hell.

Fortitude alone will not help you defeat the deep state; the deep state will bury you.

The allies of America's byzantine intelligence sector and the political partisans who steer it to their own advantage are not threatened by your quiet sense of honor. They eat that stuff up, I'm afraid. When the FBI or the CIA wants to pull political strings in favor of politicians they like, nothing helps them more than well-meaning Americans—especially conservatives—thinking they're doing their patriotic duty by believing what such agencies tell them and doing what they suggest. Former Oversight Committee chairman Rep. Trey Gowdy had to sheepishly admit to Tucker Carlson that he now regrets taking the word of the FBI and Justice Department since they made him look foolish by parroting their lies on television. Gowdy, unfortunately, proved that deference means complicity.

Former FBI director Robert Mueller certainly has fortitude. He's no loudmouthed hothead. Superficially, the determined, square-jawed, Joe Friday-like demeanor and mindset of a Mueller is exactly what traditional conservatives cherish. How fake it all turned out to be.

That's a superficial version of conservatism. Place too much naive faith in the disinterested workings of the American system of justice and in the hands of deep state insiders like Mueller and James Comey and it will roll right over you. These people want Americans to be compliant instead of unruly, quiet instead of combative. That's central to their plan to rule over us in perpetuity.

You don't stop these deep state partisans by trying to match their quiet, cold adherence to procedure. They'll win. The process is the punishment. You need to get loud and unruly and fight in an unruly way.

Fortitude—the "trust the process" faith conservatives were preaching, the soothing sounds of wait and see, as if the wheels of justice would soon render an acceptable, fair verdict if we just kept still and let them turn—fails in a situation like impeachment. Of course, by letting it play out, President Trump's presidency was nearly ruined.

Now that the impeachment farce is over, you don't recall the moments of heroic fortitude. You recall the Firebrand moments. They are memorable precisely because they are revealing.

These moments are what enabled Republicans to prevail. You may recall my colleague Rep. Mike Turner of Ohio, who in a fiery exchange during House impeachment hearings got Ambassador Gordon Sondland to admit that "nobody else on this planet told [him] that Donald Trump was tying [Ukraine] aid to these investigations" and called the assumption that Trump was pressuring Ukraine's president to investigate Joe Biden "somewhat circular."

You may also recall Rep. Elise Stefanik, Republican of New York, who tried repeatedly to get Rep. Adam Schiff to admit to blocking Republican witnesses, and asked, "Mr. Chairman, will you be prohibiting witnesses from answering members' questions, as you have in the closed-door depositions?"

Or perhaps you remember Rep. Jim Jordan questioning the integrity of the Judiciary Committee chair—or me, telling Rep. Jerry Nadler that he was out to "overturn the results of an election with unelected people." These moments were dramatic because they were substantive. You will lose every fight you don't engage.

But nothing we do in Washington would matter if there weren't a far more vibrant and interesting culture to defend beyond the Beltway. Out there, too, there are foes who won't be impressed if we behave like predictable cogs in a vast machine, doing our duty—and meekly accepting their dominance.

"Cancel culture," for example, won't be stopped by silent resolve or hoping that tech lobbyists will suddenly embrace the virtues of pluralistic debate. Our silence is exactly what they want! Like the architects of impeachment, the social justice warriors will happily thunder and pontificate about white privilege and fragility while we sit, shamefaced, waiting for them to pass judgment on us. No way! Watch footage of these clowns screaming in unison until polite, elderly professors give up and stop talking—then tell me stoic silence is the best weapon against them or that it will spur them to greater civility. I doubt it.

We have tried to be polite conservatives for the past few decades, like quiet, well-behaved children in a church pew. But the big tech companies—YouTube, Facebook, Twitter (which shadowbanned and "labeled" me)—have removed or demonetized our channels. This is the largest in-kind contribution in political history.

The blatantly biased Southern Poverty Law Center has gone from its noble origins defending civil rights to a thoroughly partisan outfit that labels inoffensive conservative, Christian, or libertarian groups as racist purveyors of "hate."

I am not, nor will I ever be, a defender of Nazis or Klansmen. I shouldn't even have to say that. But the Left throws around these sorts of smears to silence its critics and drive anyone it doesn't like out of the national conversation. These smear organizations like the SPLC should be defeated, not tolerated, except insofar as even the most reprehensible group has First Amendment rights. But we can and should denounce them. Quiet forbearance is complicity. A much more passionate response is needed. Investigations are a good first step for those who systematically libel their targets—let alone those who commit acts of violence. Attorney General Barr's large-scale investigation of left-wing terrorist group Antifa in the wake of the recent George Floyd riots is long overdue.

Democrats prefer Republicans out of power, which is to say, gelded. President George W. Bush is spoken of today by his former opponents with fondness. Why, he even sat next to Ellen DeGeneres at a Cowboys game! It's easy to forget that the Left tried to tar him as a fascist and called him "Bushitler." He was hated and vilified when in office. As former Bush speechwriter Matt Latimer recounts, Hurricane Katrina deaths were blamed on Bush's racism, war crimes in Abu Ghraib on his military viciousness, and his indulgence of Russian adventurism in the nation of Georgia on his being too friendly to Putin. Meanwhile, the Bush White House barely fought back, accepting the inevitability of the "respectable" media calling the shots and framing the arguments. Allow the Democrats to control the frame and they'll hang you every time.

But the times they are a-changing, and Trump's pugnacity in calling out the "fake news" media is his most powerful move—and a key to his enduring popularity. I know reporters, even left-wing ones, who will rethink their stories or try harder if faced with criticism by the president. Trump never surrenders the frame.

And on perhaps the most consequential issue, stoic fortitude is never likely to call into question our unconstitutional, unending wars. Fortitude—tragically, frustratingly, and almost admirably— always seems to lead to the conclusion that the only honorable course in a military quagmire is to stick it out, whether that means we're in Afghanistan another twenty years or pretending that Iraq is just another couple billion dollars away from becoming a flourishing democracy.

We conservatives have often been suckers for the argument that any criticism of neoconservative adventurism is a failure to "support the troops." That's passive acceptance of the status quo at its worst, and it gets a lot of people killed, including the troops we claim to honor.

You have to have a certain stubborn and even rebellious curiosity about these things—these policies, foreign or domestic, that have been sold to us as permanent and sacred. And these days you have to be a Firebrand to defy a deeply tortured status quo. Fortitude might have been the appropriate conservative attitude had it swept into office a President McCain, Romney, Bush, or Kasich. But under President Trump what we need is something more blazing and spirited. Fortitude means more of the same, and the same currently sucks.

For a new generation of Republican leaders to prove that President Trump isn't just a one-off, a quirk with a fleeting cult of personality, there will be a need for an animated, organized populism in our country. Not a lazy assumption that conservative values will carry the day so long as we keep saluting the flag and loving the system, or at least accepting it as given.

Washington is a corrupt place full of corrupt ambitions where few deeds serve the public. Conservative fortitude is never going to stop or even slow the corrupt machine. It's too complex to be stopped by sadly shaking our heads on national TV at anyone unpatriotic or socialist. We need to aggressively point out the countless ways Americans are being ripped off and tyrannized. We need radical and even (rhetorically) violent truth-telling in the marketplace of ideas, not the old conservative soft sell. If the Right is to prevail, it will need to start competing.

Populism can achieve this in a way the genteel wisdom of the average Bush-era country club Republican no longer can. The mindset of idle retirees is fine for idle retirees, but it won't triumph in the arena against leftists who have every major institution in our society on their side. Fighters cannot abide by the Marquess of Queensberry Rules when matched against an angry pack of rabid hyenas. Those with fortitude quietly internalize their pain. They sometimes have a high tolerance for it but a low capacity to inflict it on others.

You are in a fight when facing the Left, not a Kennedy School seminar where afterward you will all get foreign beers and celebrate how you've arrived. Every day they are coming for you. You must first come for them. Our Founders called for energy in the executive, not fortitude—toughness in the arena, not grace under pressure. Donald Trump has high energy; Jeb Bush has low energy.

Donald Trump is president. These things happen for a reason. Energy is also contagious in a way that fortitude is not.

The most dangerous thing about the do-your-duty form of conservative stoicism is that it tends to mean following orders and (famously) waiting your turn. That's an admirable quality in an actual frontline soldier but a formula for disaster in a society full of millions of citizens yearning for genuine leadership. We should raise a ruckus the technocrats can't understand or control. Remind them who's really in charge after all. Time to become a Firebrand.

This book is your invitation to the front lines of our fight. Join me with ideas, energy, images, and stories. This is not my chronological diary. You can watch me on television for that. This is how we prevail with joy—and exactly how an exciting president is leading the way against all odds.

This is not a book for those who want to grin and bear it. This book is about winning, winning so much you get sick of it. After all, isn't that what you were promised?

CHAPTER THREE

THE RUSSIA HOAX

December 9, 2017
Air Force One, en route to MAGA rally in Pensacola.

"Gaetz, what do your constituents think of this Russia bullshit?"

I was prepared for the question because my friend and one of America's best congressmen, Rep. Jamie Comer (R-KY), had been asked the same a week before and answered truthfully, telling the president, "Frankly, sir, my constituents are so happy you beat Hillary that they don't care if you did collude with Russia."

I didn't have a chance to answer because, as often happens, President Trump answered himself. You're just the audience with the president sometimes. He goes full stream of consciousness at Trump speed and in Trumpspeak. If I was annoyed at being interrupted, Trump was furious that his presidency had been interrupted before it began. The game was rigged from the start.

Now he told me, "I had nothing to do with Russia. This crap is hurting our country. I'm getting tough with China. Obama left us in horrible shape with the North Koreans. Guatemala and

Honduras must take back their illegal immigrants. I promised I'd get our freeloading allies in NATO to pay up. And all people want to bother me about is Russia."

Stream of consciousness is the best Trump because he is so clear about what he really wants and thinks. His instincts are impeccable.

It was clear to me that he wasn't going to get over it because the media never would. For all Republican Speaker Paul Ryan's hope that first year to pass the American Enterprise Institute's ten-point plan or some billionaire-donor vision of a Grand New Party with Ryan's Young Guns—all of whom were over forty-five—none of that was going to happen. The time for white papers had ended; the time for white knuckles had begun. Even if Russia wasn't the fight we picked, it was the fight we were in. Now we needed warriors, not budgeteers, to win it.

It was on Air Force One that Trump inducted me into his posse and a new band of brothers formed. We would call and text constantly. We had a standing meeting every Monday night to compare notes, congressional votes, and strategy.

The president wasn't shy about calling us by name, much the same way he did on *Fox & Friends* on April 26, 2018. He had been asked about some Republicans still lukewarm to his leader-ship style.

"Look: we have some absolute warriors. We have, I just watched your show, Jim Jordan and Mark Meadows and Matt Gaetz and DeSantis and so many…. These are all warriors. We have great people in the Republican Party."

Warriors had to be willing to make the case for the Trump presidency in any territory, on any program or platform, at any time. We had to fight, fight, fight whenever and wherever. This wasn't going to be a "kayfabe" fight, as they call staged battles like those the president had in his old gig as a WWE guest star; it was a shootout and we had to be ready to take the hits.

The president watches his haters on television and loves it when they are deboned live, on-air. He knows that his best defenders go beyond the friendly confines of Fox News to face down the likes of Chris Hayes, Chris Cuomo, and the vipers of *The View*. I've done them all. GOP Rep. Lee Zeldin of New York, one of our most cerebral congressmen, once asked why I went on so many programs with hostile hosts. "Aren't you worried they'll get you?" he asked.

"Win all your home games and go at least .500 on the road," I told Zeldin. Nobody ever became a champion ducking tough competition. Zeldin would go on to conduct his own very effective media battles. By the end of the Russia fiasco, I had faced down and exposed Peter Strzok, America's once premier counterintelligence agent. After that, *Sister Act* celebrities like Whoopi Goldberg don't seem so tough.

It has been the honor of my life to have been on this team—these Four Horsemen of justice Trump named on *Fox & Friends*, along with many others such as Rep. Devin Nunes guiding the battle. We fought every day for our president and for the voters who put him and us there, often against our own government and party.

I OFTEN THINK OF HOW THOSE OF US WHO DEFENDED THE PRESIDENT wound up in the positions of power that now determine the direction of our country and whether that is Providence's hand. It's fashionable these days to talk about reality being a "simulation," as if all of nature is reducible to whatever science fiction movie we last saw. It does seem sometimes as if there are players in the game, and then there are those who are just spectators, or, in video game parlance, "NPCs"—non-playing characters. D.C. is full of NPCs. President Trump wanted us to be players.

The rewards for stepping up have been intense. Meadows is now White House chief of staff. DeSantis is now governor of our third-most populous state. Jordan at one point served as the Republican lead on not one but two congressional committees. But we didn't know that would happen then. We ride or die with Trump, and we intended to ride. Not for nothing, the president's favorite movie is *Braveheart*, which features the line, "They may take our lives, but they'll never take our freedom!" I kid, but bands of brothers have been formed from far less.

Ryan wanted to push his lobbyist-pleasing agenda and refused to help. From health care to immigration to defending the Republican majority and president, he took failure from a hobby and made it his career. Ryan had followers in the ironically labeled "leadership" willing to tote his off-key note. Democrats sent out hundreds of subpoenas during their reign of harassment, but when we were in the majority, Speaker Ryan didn't authorize a single one. Oversight Chairman Trey Gowdy and Judiciary Committee Chairman Bob Goodlatte followed Ryan off the political cliff. Devin Nunes and the rest of us were furious, though Devin is far too much a soft-spoken gentleman to admit that now.

Gowdy, a tough former federal prosecutor, never liked President Trump. Gowdy and I both lived in our Capitol offices, and we used the gym frequently at night. He told me he resented that Trump never granted him an interview for the job he wanted: attorney general. My talks with Gowdy never extended to the open-air congressional showers, though. Gowdy was the only male member of Congress known to shower exclusively in the private, handicapped enclosure.

President Trump once exclaimed to me, "Devin Nunes has balls!"—holding both hands out as if they held two grapefruits. Something tells me the same cannot be said for Trey.

Nunes had created the marquee witness list to expose the Russia hoax early, before more harm could be done to America: Comey, Brennan, Clapper, Rice...all the deep state names you now know as premeditated traitors. Ryan then "directed" Gowdy and Goodlatte, as chairmen of the Oversight and Judiciary Committees, to perform the investigation. Sadly, it was *all* performance and *zero* investigation.

While Goodlatte said little (he is a man with very little to say), Gowdy couldn't stop talking. And his words hurt our quest for justice. On May 29, 2018, he appeared on *The Story with Martha MacCallum* after emerging from a closed-door meeting with Speaker Ryan, FBI Acting Director/apologist Christopher Wray, and Deputy AG Rod Rosenstein (as I write, Wray still holds his position at the FBI, although I suspect he won't be there in a second Trump term). Gowdy declared on MacCallum's show, "I am even more convinced that the FBI did exactly what their fellow citizens would want them to do when they got the information they got—and that it has nothing to do with Donald Trump."

Gowdy's defense of the deep state was devastating. He gave the FBI a cleansing cat bath before the nation. In every interview Jim Jordan, Mark Meadows, or I did subsequently, we would be confronted with Gowdy's embrace of those attacking the president. "What do you know that Trey Gowdy doesn't?" we were asked incessantly.

Momentum was lost. Crooks in our own government escaped and suffered only the tepid indictment of government reports, not grand juries.

On May 14, 2019, I called for the release of sworn interview transcripts from the Intelligence Committee. Almost a year to the day later, they were released. They exposed that all along Trey Gowdy had known about the lack of legitimate predicate for the Russia hoax. He knew it when he took interviews with potential witnesses and got responses in 2017—and when he scuttled our work in 2018.

Gowdy would later sheepishly admit his "mistake" during an interview on *Tucker Carlson Tonight*, enjoying post-Congress life as a Fox News contributor. Little good it does us now. He had let the voters down and allowed a scam to continue. History should judge him harshly for his failure to judge the facts honestly.

At the time, what the Democrats couldn't do electorally, they had to do antidemocratically. Donald Trump was victorious, but he still had the haters and the losers to contend with, and some were ensconced in the federal government. Some of them were even appointed by him. Personnel is policy, but in the rush during Russiagate, many positions were not given the careful attention they deserved and were instead filled by people the establishment recommended and whom the Trump team gambled they could trust.

This, too, was by design. Taking President Trump's attention away from his duties, they wound up disrupting the flow of his presidency. FBI background checks dragged on for languid weeks and months. Leaks of sensitive information were frequent and vicious, and not always true.

Everybody was handwringing and bedwetting as if it were all Watergate to justify the obsessive focus on Russian collusion. They even brought back some of the Watergate cast of characters, including disgraced CNN commentator John Dean, though this bunch's second act was less Watergate 2.0 and more like *Grumpier Old Men*.

To be honest, I don't think many Americans could find Russia on a map, even if people joked that Sarah Palin said that she could see it from her porch. While the globalist Left might see that as a criticism, I see it as an indication of how far we've come. My parents did nuclear attack drills at their schools, feeling the ever-present tension of the world's most dangerous game of chicken. We don't care now because we don't have to care. George W. Bush thought he could see into Putin's soul, John McCain thought he saw the KGB in there, and Mitt Romney saw the crippling former empire as our greatest geopolitical foe. Okay, boomers.

Russia has never mattered less in my lifetime. Its two main exports are models and oil, and America has plenty of both. When was the last time you used a Russian product? Russia is never either as strong or as weak as she looks, however, and she may yet prove to be more dangerous on her way down to demographic ruination than she was on her way up to communist dominion.

I have been on many television broadcast shows—it's hard *not* to see me if you watch enough TV. But you will never see me interviewed on Russia Today, that modern-day version of *Pravda*. I believe Russia belongs not in the future but the past and that her ailing economy and oligarchic politics reflect that growing realization. Everybody who can is trying to get out of Russia—with whatever cash or arms they can launder through British, French, or Swiss property markets.

It isn't quite the end of history. I don't believe Russia or her satellites will become good neoliberals tomorrow or maybe ever. As Russia weakens, the line between state action and criminal thuggery all but disappears. At least they no longer pretend to have a compelling, competing vision of the world beyond raw power and thievery, though. Seen another way, the KGB may be all that is holding Russia together and preventing its oblivion.

To be sure, gangsters can still imperil our security. Just look at the chaos south of our own border. But the cartels have something Americans want and some even need to buy—drugs. We don't need Russia quite as desperately.

But the condition of the country isn't why the Washington intelligence and media elite want a conflict with Russia. Washington wants a new Cold War because the Cold War was good for Washington. Cold wars are better than hot wars because you don't even have to make sure the weapons work. Imagine majoring in Russian back in the 1980s only to learn shortly afterward that the Berlin Wall had fallen. There's no on-the-job retraining for bureaucrats and policy experts, comrade. For many in Washington, long ago trained to address one specific big problem, the Cold War will only end when their bodies are cold. Progress in foreign policy too often advances funeral to funeral.

How to react to Robert Mueller's appointment as independent special counsel was the subject of much debate in the Republican conference at the time the Russia investigation began. Ryan and Gowdy both surmised that Mueller was some sort of Beltway paladin. The thinking went that we should all praise Mueller, confirm the legitimacy of his team's investigative work, and then pray that Trump hadn't done anything criminal. Besides, they thought, a President Pence—one of Congress's own—wouldn't be so bad sitting in the Oval Office if it came to that. What couldn't be done at the ballot box—defeating Trump—could be accomplished ex post facto in the witness box.

The Russia hoax not only debased Congress and harmed the presidency but it also distracted us from the real threat—namely China. Search your own home and count the things you own that were made in China. And you bought these things when relations were a lot better than they are now. Asia's largest consumer of energy, China, is right next to Asia's largest producer, Russia.

They are building bridges to one another that could well imperil the free world.

We can beat Russia and other fossil fuel foes just by keeping the price of oil perpetually low. But don't take my word for it. Ronald Reagan did just that, as Steven Hayward recounts in *The Age of Reagan: The Conservative Counterrevolution, 1980–1989*. It was a deliberate policy of the Reagan administration to bankrupt petrostates even if it wound up hurting Oklahoma and Texas. Never again would Americans wait in line to fuel their cars and go to work. We should finish the job.

The Stone Age didn't end because we ran out of stones. The Coal Age didn't end because we ran out of coal. Nor will the Oil Age end because we have run out of oil. Peak oil is a fantasy. Conservatives decry the Green New Deal because they rightly understand it as a socialist wish list, not a sane way to end our reliance on fossil fuels. Stewardship is not socialism, though, and we should indeed be doing what we can to husband our precious resources before they are gone forever, and think about replacements while we do so.

China is rising while Russia sinks. Even when China mimics Western-style capitalism, it does so with an authoritarian tinge. SenseTime tracks your face. BGI steals your genetics. DJI spies on you from the sky. The end goal of China is to make us all, like too much of China's Uighur population, suspects under house arrest.

But criticism of Russia and China should not blind us to our own errors. We become like our enemies all too quickly when we think the ends justify the means. In the case of the establishment's no-holds-barred war on Trump, the Bill of Rights very quickly became just a suggestion. Every civil liberty was thrown out the window in the effort to bring down the president. Baseless surveillance? No problem! Weird federal informants? No big deal! Planting fake stories? Of course! Convincing other countries to illegally monitor Americans? Absolutely cool. Changing evidence before a secret court? Why not! Attempting to entrap members of the president's family and campaign? How exciting.

And the sick thing is that they thought they were ending American liberties to protect America. How quickly we do wickedness when we justify what's wrong.

The Obama administration blamed Russia for its failures rather than its own stupidity. Scapegoating, as I suggested earlier, makes things easier emotionally. You don't have to accept responsibility for, say, having told Russia on a hot mic that you'll have "more flexibility" after the next election, so they shouldn't worry too much about conservative hardliners here. On the other hand, you also don't have to accept responsibility for expanding wars you said you'd end or starting a few new ones along the way.

Obama's foreign policy misadventures needed scapegoats, and so his team would do anything to make the picture of Russia as an equal power to the U.S. appear true. The Obama team was also too proud to believe that they were outsmarted in an election by Donald Trump. We must have been defeated by the Russians, and they had to be underhanded to get it done! A cabal formed at the top of our government to shift the blame for Hillary Clinton's defeat, and that effort included President Obama's closest allies. The recently declassified notes of disgraced former FBI agent and Trump hater Peter Strzok prove that it was Vice President Biden himself who suggested the never-before-used Logan Act to set up General Michael Flynn. Biden had a central role in the Obama era's corruption. Like the autocratic foreign rulers they so often condemned, they deployed tactics that should never have been used on American soil.

We now know that on the final day of the Obama administration—the same day when I sat in the bleachers watching the president take the oath of office—the outgoing national security advisor, Susan Rice, was sending emails about the Obama group's stay-behind contingency plan for coping with a Trump presidency they did not see coming, did not want, and would do everything to thwart.

Stalin's security enforcer Lavrenti Beria, ironically, was the person who said, in a brazen show of elite corruption, "Show me the man, and I'll show you the crime"—meaning that a sufficiently corrupt investigation can concoct almost anything about anyone. Since the British intelligence consultant Christopher Steele had indeed built the so-called "Trump dossier" largely out of disinformation created by anti-Trump donors and Russia itself, the case against Trump had more in common with KGB-style pressure tactics than did the intensely American, very non-stealthy Trump campaign itself. It still amazes me that the media believed the Trump campaign was able to keep up a criminal conspiracy with Russia when they couldn't even keep a secret about their own campaign-inspired sexual hijinks. (Don't judge. Every campaign has some.)

The anti-Trump plotters had a perfect scapegoat in Gen. Michael Flynn, a former Democrat who had publicly joined the calls for Hillary Clinton to be prosecuted. Having served in the Obama administration, Flynn was a traitor in his former colleagues' eyes and had to be punished severely. His crime was merely behaving as Washingtonians always do once out of office: he wanted to monetize his time in a new way after exiting the military.

With Flynn as the primary target, the man putting the Russia hoax into action was FBI Director James Comey, who Trump—depicted as partisan and paranoid by Democrats—was trusting enough to keep around until May 2017. Trump thought, like many Americans, that the nation's police and intelligence agencies had a certain code of honor that helped them rise above politics and methodically seek the truth. No such luck, as Trump increasingly grew aware. A disinterested, professional government doesn't exist.

I suspect that even a political brawler like Trump found it hard to believe, prior to his first term in office, that the Democrats and deep state agencies would disgrace themselves with the kind of dirty tricks they were deploying. At its heart, starting slightly *before* Trump won the election, the plan was to use thinly sourced or outright fictitious accusations of collusion between his staff and Russia as a pretext to further investigate the Trump campaign. The investigation would then go right on into the new president's first term. There would be no "honeymoon period" for this president, but there would be plenty of acrimony.

If you thought the president's marriage to Marla Maples was bumpy, his presidency would prove to be a very wild ride. It was as if a spying maid had been left in the household by a disgruntled ex-wife to dig up dirt on her successor—including any contact, however trivial, between Team Trump and anyone with current or former ties to Russia. Thus Dr. Carter Page was gussied up as a potential Russian agent to enable otherwise baseless surveillance, despite the fact that our own intelligence community was debriefing a cooperative Page following contacts with Russians.

But once Team Trump was under the Obama/Comey spying regime, any forgotten or half-remembered brush with an Eastern European would now be twisted into a verdict of treason—with an obliging press braying its Putin paranoia each night.

Americans tend to trust the federal agencies tasked with enforcing the law, and it became an easy strategy for the Democrats to paint themselves as patient people who just wanted to see what the investigation turned up, even as they fanned the flames of anti-Trump hatred, encouraging the narrative that a man who might be a double agent in thrall to a foreign power was now sitting in the Oval Office.

On May 9, 2018, Trump carved a cancer out of the FBI when he fired James Comey. I got the news while in the Balkans with a bipartisan delegation of the Judiciary Committee. It felt odd lecturing new nations on the importance of a professional and fair judicial system as our president was having to fire the FBI director.

I spent most of the trip with David Cicilline (D-RI). David is a gay former mob lawyer who served as mayor of Providence before entering Congress. One must be smart and tough to be a gay mob lawyer, I figured. David is both. Everyone else on the trip brought a spouse, so David was my platonic travel buddy. We both understood that upon returning to Washington, the fight over the legitimacy of the Trump presidency would be on, and we would each be called to it. Despite our fiery ways and opposing views, we remain friends.

In the days and weeks that followed, Trump's fellow Republicans could have risen to his defense. Canning Comey was delivering on the promise to "drain the swamp!" It turns out, though, some of the alligators were going to miss him.

The calm, above-the-fray posture of some establishment Republicans made it easier for them to wait instead of pressing the strategic advantage. For those of us who were frustrated, chomping at the bit to make good on our promise of a populist rebellion, it looked as if party leadership might be just as happy if Trump were removed. The only thing permanent in Washington is sloth.

Media and establishment figures on both sides extolled Mueller's professionalism and low-key objectivity. His biography was endlessly covered so that you didn't look too closely at what he was doing. Meanwhile, Mueller's team was shaking down Gen. Flynn, who had briefly become Trump's national security advisor, threatening to prosecute his son for minor offenses unless Flynn himself pled guilty to "lying" to investigators. The goal of such moves was never justice but the creation of pressure on Trump's associates to get them to "roll" on their boss.

While I've never met Flynn, it's clear he's a fan of my work. On several occasions, he would send me direct messages via Twitter with cryptic slogans and images that seemingly encouraged me to keep fighting.

Meanwhile, as media leftists like Rachel Maddow warned nightly that the republic was imperiled, establishment Republicans judiciously "waited to see" what Mueller's team—stacked with partisan Democrats—would turn up.

Russiagate was a pivotal example of that passive Beltway conservatism that turns, inevitably, into the maintenance of business as usual. Just as many members would rather let an executive agency promulgate a new rule to avoid actual lawmaking, so could play-it-safe Republicans claim they were "waiting to see the results of Mueller's investigation" before weighing in for or against their president.

That isn't what we are called to do. Our voters expect us to have our own views, as a coequal branch of government. The separation of powers requires us to think seriously about our duties. Fence-sitting and cowardice are often dressed up as prudence and judicious respect for due process. This passive-aggressive approach to opposing Trump and his populist voters permeates the conservative movement, or at least the Republican Party.

WHAT BEGAN DURING THE ELECTION WITH THE MISGUIDED Twitter hashtag #NeverTrump, used by Republicans who thought they could somehow pressure their party into picking a different standard-bearer, later became a lasting mini-movement of obsolete yet influential "Never Trump" Republicans who would continue to praise Mueller, posture as champions of the rule of law, and find ever-new excuses to fawn over Democrats until Mueller finally delivered his mild, confused, and anti-climactic report.

The #NeverTrumpers promoted their hashtag much as they had promoted the Iraq War and its chaotic aftermath: by repeatedly lying and demonizing anyone who disagreed. If they had their way, we'd be in dozens of wars right now. The faction's ringleaders included former Bush administration officials William Kristol and David Frum, hated for years by Democrats for defending George W. Bush but now lionized as the "conscience" of the Republican Party. George F. Will, once considered the "dean" of American conservative journalists, also threw in his lot with these unemployed Bush-era holdovers.

While the Trumps had promised we'd get sick of winning, the #NeverTrumpers never tired of losing. I once heard Ivanka Trump share her perspective on this sad batch of loser Republicans. We were riding with her father and brother in the presidential limousine, the famous "Beast." "They either lose elections, are totally forgotten, or they get a job on CNN/MSNBC," she dispassionately observed.

Some were still in Congress, though, hiding in plain sight behind the speaker's rostrum.

With Mueller as a malleable masthead, Attorney General Jeff Sessions recused from everything save his own dithering weakness, and Deputy AG Rod Rosenstein a secret member of the Resistance, the special counsel's team of partisans effectively had unbridled power. They used their nascent evidentiary foundation for maximum political effect.

They indicted never-to-be-seen-or-heard-from Russians, harassed innocent members of the First Family, busted Roger Stone for accidentally guessing right about WikiLeaks disclosures, drove up massive legal bills for administration officials, and found out that Paul Manafort was up to no good back in the '80's.

Not exactly a bargain at roughly $40 million for a taxpayer-funded coup attempt.

Rather than punish these rogue agents, the media empowered them, touting their mendacious books, and even going so far as to promote their crowdfunded legal expenses. Former CIA director John Brennan was allowed to bloviate about the Trump/Russia nonsense nightly on CNN.

Of course, we now know that Brennan said one thing on television and another under oath. TV-Brennan declared Trump "treasonous" and "in the pocket of Putin." Sworn witness-Brennan sheepishly admitted that there was no basis to allege criminal conspiracy.

Obama-era DNI James Clapper was no better. On CNN, Clapper accused Trump of "essentially aiding and abetting the Russians." But under oath in 2017, he admitted he "never saw any direct empirical evidence that the Trump campaign or someone in it was plotting/conspiring with the Russians to meddle with the election."

Whether Brennan, Clinton, or Obama should be considered the real instigator of all this is debatable. But Joe Biden at least acknowledges he was in the room while Obama was discussing how to hand off the Trump investigation to FBI Director Comey after the administration exited. So even sleepy Joe can't be let off the hook (assuming he remembers he even worked in the White House).

In truth, Biden was one of some dozen Obama officials who were in on the decision to "unmask" surveilled Trump campaign figures—naming them in shared transcripts regardless of whether warrants or charges were being pursued and in the process gaining useful partisan intel on Trump's allies. All regarded Trump as a dangerous interloper to be stopped by any means necessary.

You get a sense of this urgency in the 2017 film *The Final Year*. The film chronicles the final moments of the Obama administration when the us-versus-them attitude of the globalist administration is laid bare. The unseen enemy is all those nations who just won't go along with the optimistic, neoliberal worldview the Obama foreign policy team chants as a mantra. The chief foe for them is Russia—ironic, considering their assiduous efforts to "reset" U.S.-Russian relations.

"The Russian Federation doesn't care about atrocities committed against people.... When Putin wakes up in the morning, he doesn't think, 'How can I prevent mass atrocities today?' " said former Obama official (and bestselling author) Samantha Power. Power would later lie to Congress about how often she had unmasked Americans named in foreign intelligence reports, including, of course, Michael Flynn. "Are you truly incapable of shame?" Power asked of Russia before the UN General Assembly. "Is there literally nothing that can shame you?" We should ask her—and her publisher—the same question.

Watching *The Final Year*, it's easy to see why so many of the Obama staff worked so hard to preserve the gains they thought they had made. "Putin doesn't pursue Russia's interests," said Ben Rhodes. "He pursues Putin's interests." It would similarly be in the interests of the Obama regime to do all they could to oppose Trumpism, especially if (unable to understand him any other way) they thought of Trump as just another self-serving autocrat. "Any thought that any of us might have had that we could go gently into the night, that thought has been vanquished," Power said. "So we're in this for the long, long haul."

To some of us in that fateful spring of 2017, it looked as if the Republicans weren't even going to fight back. For too long, they seemed content to let the Mueller investigation take its course without turning the magnifying glass back on the investigators themselves, and the cozy network of politicians and intelligence/ DOJ operatives behind them.

DURING MY FIRST YEAR IN CONGRESS, MY BEST FRIENDS WORKED in the Atlanta Airport, Hartsfield. There was no direct flight from my district to Washington then, so Hartsfield is where I spent much of my free time. One July 2017 layover, I called my mentor, Rep. Jim Jordan of Ohio. "Aren't you tired of just taking punches in the face, Jim?" I asked. "I've got a plan to raise our fists and start swinging back. Wanna hear it?" He did.

Jim Jordan is Congress's most talented and hardest-working member. Like me, he is not a patient man. He is that rare combination of someone who both honorably serves in Congress and actually likes serving in Congress. A national champion collegiate wrestler and legit political Firebrand himself, Jordan once told me that the reason he loved the job was that every day was a chance to compete hard for something to help people. If I couldn't convince Jordan, my plan was going nowhere.

"Why is only Trump facing a special counsel? We all know Hillary was using the Clinton Foundation as her international money-laundering operation. We know this 'dossier' is Russian interference fueled by the Democrats. Let's come out for a special counsel to investigate them too!"

Jordan bit the line so hard I almost had to readjust the drag. He was all in to turn up the heat. Reps. Ron DeSantis, Mark Meadows, Andy Biggs, Mike Johnson, Raul Labrador, and many others soon joined. The last Republican Judiciary Committee member to join our new offensive game plan was Chairman Goodlatte. When the letter finally went to Attorney General Sessions calling for parity in the special counsel game, Goodlatte placed it above his signature. We had dislodged the cemented Republican establishment, if only for a moment.

Soon, though, a frustrated Trump noticed a few of us were now eager to stop playing defense and fight back against the phony proceedings. It was time to make some noise in the congressional hearings about it all instead of just sitting there like a bunch of worried defendants told by their lawyer not to testify on their own behalf. It's not just that this quiet tactic tends to make your side look guilty. It also means you're not pointing out wrongdoing on the other side. Time to go on offense. Silence is stupidity is complicity.

It was clear that the anti-Trump forces were willing to try winning the whole struggle through innuendo even if it went nowhere in court. Denigrate, then destroy, but never debate.

No longer limited by any rules of decorum that might have restrained her while still in the White House, former national security advisor Susan Rice, no doubt taking her cue from powerful friends like Obama and Hillary Clinton, said on ABC News in July 2017 of Trump:

> "He's taken a series of steps that, had Vladimir Putin dictated them, [Trump] couldn't have mirrored more effectively. What his motivations are, I think is a legitimate question, one that the Special Counsel is investigating, but the policies this president has pursued globally have served Vladimir Putin's interests in dividing the West, undermining democracy."

Here's a question for Rice: Is it not undermining democracy for an unelected group of bureaucrats to decide what can and can't be done by the next president?

Her main argument in closed-door hearings was that Trump allies such as Flynn kept downplaying the Russian threat, calling it a declining power, and describing China as a rising danger—as indeed it is! But maybe it was Trump's frequent campaign talk of getting tough with China in trade negotiations that really freaked them out. China is not only rising in importance relative to Russia, but it also—as recent events have made clear—has its tentacles deep inside the American business, academic, and political establishment, where it has spread around millions of dollars. China's apologists include venture capitalists like Mike Moritz of Sequoia (which backed Google!) and *New York Times* columnists like Thomas Friedman, who openly envy China's authoritarian leftism.

Establishment Republicans, for their part, were equally wary of Trump's potential to rock the boat. I think some were genuinely unsure how they wanted to see the Mueller investigation play out. Many were content to roll the dice and avoid staking out a strong position on the merits of the underlying evidence.

It was an unholy if convenient alliance between Democrats, establishment Republicans, and the Permanent Washington bureaucracy. At the time Mueller was appointed, Speaker Ryan, Rep. Gowdy, and Sen. Lindsey Graham all supported the appointment of a special counsel, with Graham (later to become a fiery critic of the Democrats' impeachment circus) assuring the public that the Mueller investigation was "not a witch hunt." Trust the process, they all said. But the process was the punishment and the political outcome desired.

For my part, I viewed Mueller's appointment as an attempt to put a legalistic gloss on a political attack upon the president, done with the help of establishment Republicans like Goodlatte.

By the time he left office in 2019, Goodlatte—elected in 1992—had been chair of the Judiciary Committee for six years and, in the mid-2000s, chair of the powerful House Agriculture Committee for four. You don't serve as the chairman of not one but two congressional committees if you don't blindly follow leadership. The warriors quickly realized that dealing with Goodlatte was worthless.

I wasn't going to just sit back and let gridlock carry the day. For a populist revolt to fizzle out in ambiguous legal proceedings would be one of the saddest letdowns in the history of our democracy. Those of us who had been willing to fight to get Trump and his allies into office were now spoiling for a fight on the House floor. Behind the scenes, Trump, who understands stagecraft, looked forward to seeing what we could do.

Republican Reps. Louie Gohmert of Texas, Jordan, Nunes, Meadows, Biggs, and others emerged as the new class of fighters. Starting in the summer of 2017, we openly said that no collusion had been proven with anything like normal legal standards. We called out the investigation as something that had become an end unto itself, a club with which to beat up President Trump, not an honest attempt to unearth the details of any known or seriously suspected crime.

Trump's defenders were determined to draw attention to the heavy-handed tactics of the investigators themselves, and I think this contributed to the very cautious, almost softball tone of a defeated-looking Mueller's eventual report in 2019. That report acknowledged, albeit with many weasel words, what a few of us had always known: no evidence of serious wrongdoing was found.

Mueller's testimony remains the most-watched moment in recent political history. An astonishing 22 million tuned in. The press had mythologized Mueller as the embodiment of virtue, honesty, and strength. Fifteen Republicans and the Clinton-Democrat machine couldn't take out Donald Trump, but Mueller could—or so they hoped.

After reviewing every moment of testimony Mueller had given Congress over a multi-decade career, I could see why they were bullish. The man was downright steely. On the day of the hearing, I half expected Mueller to ride in on a lightning bolt, hurling spears of fire at the committee. The reality was much different.

Mueller's team had leaked in the days before the hearing that he wasn't all there—that calling him would be a mistake for Democrats. In late-night prep sessions with my fellow Republicans, I passionately preached not to believe it. "Mueller has been preparing for twelve hours a day to embarrass us all!" I exclaimed. "He'll be the best we've ever seen, so we better be our best."

Whoops. From Judiciary Chairman Jerry Nadler's opening questions it was clear Mueller wasn't playing with a full deck. He seemed old, confused, distracted, at times not seeming to know what was in his own report. Even softball questions from the Democrats stumped him. Mueller's testimony looked more like elder abuse in progress than the culmination of a fair investigation.

For a moment, I felt sorry for him. But the moment quickly passed.

With their whole case resting on the sandpile of cheap insinuations that was the Steele dossier, I put it to Mueller like this at one point in the hearings, when he tried to claim that validating the Steele dossier wasn't his "purview": "No, it is exactly your purview, Mr. Mueller, and here's why. Only one of these two things is possible: either Steele made this whole thing up and there were never any Russians telling him of this vast criminal conspiracy that you didn't find—or Russians lied to Steele."

"As I said before and I'll say again, it's not my purview, as others are investigating what you address," Mueller told me feebly.

Mueller's testimony was a dud and it left Democrats bitter and demoralized. After months of daily assurances from Maddow and a foolish press that Mueller would "destroy" Trump, they had, instead, destroyed their own credibility.

Yet the investigation mania would return with the sudden shift to the topic of Ukraine. The same gang that had clung for two years to a failed Hillary Clinton campaign had a new phony outrage to flog—and they were now looking to defend the new establishment champion: Joe Biden.

CHAPTER FOUR

A PERFECT CALL

December 19, 2019
The White House. Private residence. Evening.

THE TOWERING PRESIDENT EXTENDED HIS ARM, POINTING AS IF to amplify the history lesson he was giving.

"He wrote the Gettysburg Address right over there," Trump told a few of us on a visit to the White House. "Lincoln was very melancholy. We would call it depressed today. Melancholy sounds more elegant. Everything was going wrong for the guy. His son died. His wife was not right. Worst of all, he kept losing. At the beginning of the Civil War, he lost and lost—all the early battles. He almost lost the country! Then he put a great general in charge—Ulysses S. Grant. Everyone told Lincoln that Grant was crazy. He drank too much. He used bad language. He was a real son of a bitch. A butcher. But Grant was a winner."

President Lincoln once said of Grant, "I cannot spare this man. He fights."

Grant knew that to defeat Lee he didn't need beautiful formations but men grinding away at their objective, come what may. Preserving the Union required nothing less than total focus and devotion.

Like Lincoln, Trump also cultivates a team of rivals, but tonight the band of brothers—and one sister—could be permitted a bit of R and R. President Trump turned to the small group of guests that included Reps. Mark Meadows, Jim Jordan, Andy Biggs, Debbie Lesko, Mike Johnson, and their spouses. All had joined for the White House Christmas party. My date was there too—way out of my league, as the president delighted in telling me in front of her.

"Lincoln had the great General Grant...and I have Matt Gaetz!" (She was impressed, though perhaps not that much. There wouldn't be a second date.)

Some presidents didn't allow their own vice president in the White House residence. Trump has his friends over enough to have their mail sent to 1600 Pennsylvania Ave. He gives tours and tells stories with the gusto and pageantry of a true showman. The Lincoln Bedroom is his favorite attraction. The House Judiciary Committee had voted out articles of impeachment earlier that day. We were in the middle of the fight for the Trump presidency. It was a fight we were winning, and we knew it. All smiles.

Days later, the left-leaning *Guardian* newspaper would begrudgingly publish: "So far, all impeachment has done is make Donald Trump more popular." Indeed, Trump has an inhuman ability to absorb the most vicious attacks and turn them to his advantage. Impeachment, once considered the gravest of choices for Congress, was now just the same old politics by different, more destructive means.

Donald Trump is still America's president. Impeachment over Trump's communication with Ukraine was a frivolous distraction—an exorcism of sorts for Democrats who, immediately after their election loss and failed Russia investigation, still needed an outlet for the Trump Derangement Syndrome warping their electorally, if not eternally, damned souls. In the end, the constitutional system of checks and balances worked. But win a few battles though we may, understand this: they will never stop coming after him—or us.

As recently as May 18, 2020, long after the last echoes of #UkraineFirst bureaucrats and #AmericaLast liberal law professors had faded, House Democrats were *still* filing pleadings asserting an active impeachment investigation remains underway. If they spent half the time legislating that they spend investigating, Americans would have better roads, cleaner air, and better health care. But it isn't about the American people to the radical Left—it is about power and power at all costs. Trump shocked the world by taking control from the elites of Permanent Washington. They wanted it back. They still do. And they may yet get it. In politics, there are neither permanent defeats nor permanent victories. We must keep fighting.

To quit is to admit their defeat. They can't abandon the strategy of trying to delegitimize President Trump and our movement, because they've seen that they can't beat us in fair debates, open hearings, or fraud-free presidential elections. Politics used to be "win the argument, win the vote," but if the vote can be subverted and overturned, well, why participate politically? Better to demonize, denigrate, and destroy than debate.

The Russia hoax was born of Obama's train-wreck foreign policy and Hillary's failed candidacy. The straight-to-DVD Ukrainian impeachment sequel followed the scuttled Russia hoax. Had they succeeded with Russia, you better believe you wouldn't know the name of any Ukrainian president or prosecutor—not unless you were Joe Biden keeping track of familial kickbacks.

In the fights still to come, remember: Speaker Pelosi doesn't lack political skill. Her strategy and tactics changed from Russia to Ukraine. They continue changing. We didn't beat her then and won't beat the radical Left now by gently lecturing in dulcet tones that people on our side should contain their "outrage." We were at our best when we were on offense—like General Grant!

Every part of the swamp wants its shot at our president. First, the FBI failed with the Russia hoax, then the State Department crowd in Foggy Bottom failed with the Ukraine hoax. Impeachment proves that conservatives lose when we wait and see. We win when we take bold action and hit back hard—harder than they do.

I wasn't on the Judiciary Committee just to politely take lectures from law professors who couldn't win an election for the Mosquito Control Board but whose hatred for President Trump triggered their anti-democratic impulses. I wasn't sleeping on a cot in the Longworth Office Building four nights a week so some #AmericaLast Georgetown School of Foreign Service graduates could substitute their foreign-funded "studied" judgment for that of those of us who had successfully earned the trust of American voters. That's not how it works when America is at her best.

The Ukraine saga taught us how we must keep fighting in the era of Trump: unapologetically, sometimes loudly, with all we've got.

It started with what President Trump would later dub "a perfect call."

September 25, 2019
The White House. Roosevelt Room.

THE *WALL STREET JOURNAL* HAD EXPLOSIVE REPORTING. President Trump had, on eight occasions, directly and explicitly threatened the president of Ukraine, they alleged. Either fork over dirt on Biden to help me win an election, or I'll withhold the weapons you want, so the story went. The *Journal* said a transcript existed of the call. A whistleblower had firsthand evidence!

I was about to learn that none of it was true.

About a dozen senators and representatives sat nervously under the portrait of Theodore Rex, raised up on his magnificent horse in obvious triumph of some kind. We were young and old. Male and female. Moderates and right-wingers. Our commonality was that we had been selected by the White House to review the Trump-Zelensky phone call transcript for the first time. We were the supporters the president knew he needed on the front lines, going line by line.

"The reporting is false," said White House Counsel Pat Cipollone as he handed out the transcript. "The president is going to be releasing this transcript today. Once people see it, this should all go away. I honestly don't get what all the fuss is about." Pat is a brilliant legal mind but, like the rest of us, he clearly misjudged the power of an unquenched craving for impeachment.

Sen. Ron Johnson is a Ukraine policy encyclopedia. After several minutes of group silent reading, he blurted out, "This is it? This is nothing. We've been trying to get Ukraine to clean up their act for years. President Trump was reinforcing what Republicans and Democrats have been working towards with Zelensky. He's obviously looking out for our country."

About time, if you ask me. Senators Barack Obama and Chuck Hagel spent billions of your dollars in the Ukraine, that most corrupt of European countries, to pay the Ukrainians not to arm up. Rather hilariously, the senators offered the same deal to Russia, which wisely realized that if Ukraine disarmed, Russia could just take what it wanted from them. And that is exactly what ended up happening.

Democrats, who once joined Senator Ron Johnson in signing bipartisan letters urging action against rampant corruption in Ukraine, would soon act as if the place were the Garden of Eden, free of all sin. They suddenly contended it was ridiculous and possibly criminal for heightened investigations into dirty deeds in the former Soviet satellite state. Trump asking President Zelensky to help was tantamount to treason!

Goldman Sachs labeled Ukraine the third-most corrupt country in the world in which to do business. It's a big world, with lots of corrupt places. International money flows through Ukraine in—shall we say—odd ways. To attack a U.S. president for asking why is insane.

Several Biden allies and former Obama administration intelligence operatives on the call sensed a potential threat to the establishment's brand-new (yet quite old) Great White Hope, Joe Biden. As Biden appeared likely to become the Democratic presidential nominee, these hacks couldn't just sit back and do nothing while they watched a campaign liability created out of Biden's son, Hunter, who had sat on the board of a Ukrainian energy company called Burisma—the very company under a corruption inquiry spotlight.

Hunter Biden's Ukrainian influence-peddling racket wasn't a secret to the Obama/Biden posse or really to anyone in Washington. When Ambassador Marie Yovanovitch was preparing for confirmation hearings, the "Hunter issue" was given particular attention. George Kent, an anti-Trump witness from the State Department, confessed that Burisma's corruption warranted even more investigation. He had America's embassy pull out of a joint venture with Burisma over corruption concerns.

Are we really supposed to believe that a corrupt Ukrainian company, under investigation, hired Hunter Biden because of his talent rather than his access? Not even Hunter Biden believes that. In an ABC interview, he candidly said that he probably wouldn't have gotten the job but for his last name. There are plenty of Americans who benefit from a good surname. I sure have. But we don't use our good names to bleed cash from bad, corrupt foreign companies while our dad is vice president.

"I did nothing wrong—and I'll never do it again" would functionally be the confusing response from Biden.

Minority Leader McCarthy chimed in next. "What will the media say? He did mention Biden. That isn't great."

"It was a perfect call!" The president's voice shot out of the speakerphone. The president is always his own best communications director and hype man. He was right. We agreed that the media would look foolish for, as they typically do, exaggerating. Rep. Schiff would likely slither away following the disclosure, humiliated again so soon after Russia. Pelosi would move on to her next attempt to virtue signal. We had overestimated their sense of honor and underestimated their sensitivity to shame. Evidence or not, they decided the impeachment show must go on! There was no other act or agenda from the Democrats.

"Russia" had died with Muller looking more like someone who escaped a nursing home memory ward than the Trump slayer that the Democrats and their allies in the Fake News media had advertised. Ukraine would emerge now as the "go-for-broke" impeachment strategy, evidence be damned. We do stupid things when we are desperate.

October 23, 2019
House Intelligence Committee. Secure Compartmentalized
Information Facility (SCIF).

"Mr. Gaetz has returned," I overheard a staff member whisper to Adam Schiff. Much to my surprise, I had been thrown out of the SCIF days before. I assumed because the Judiciary Committee has principal jurisdiction over impeachment—and since they were impeaching my president—that I'd be able to at least observe. Not so. Well, screw that. This time I brought backup.

About fifty House Republicans and I had just held a press conference lambasting the Democrats' secret impeachment-related proceedings going on within this "Secret Compartmentalized Information Facility."

At this point, Speaker Pelosi had seen enough of the bumbling, disheveled Rep. Jerry Nadler in Judiciary Committee proceedings. It was like a line change in hockey it was so instantaneous. Judiciary Democrats had been benched, and the Intelligence Committee had subbed in. You only change the lineup if you are losing. After Russia, they were.

During Russia, Democrats always believed they were "one shoe-drop" away from a massive swing in public opinion that never happened. Try as they might, nothing seemed to work. Michael Cohen! Roger Stone indicted! Manafort and Gates! A Russian troll farm! Nobody cared. While President Trump focused on provisions for the American people, the Democrats couldn't stop spinning fiction about distant lands. To many of my hardworking constituents, it was like, Russia…Ukraine…what's next? Are they going to accuse Trump of colluding with Narnia?

From Comey's fake diary leaks to the unmasking of Gen. Flynn, the Russia hoax strategy was to get information out as fast as possible, to feed their narrative. That failed. Now, they were going to take their time, but time is dangerous to fraudsters. In the Ukraine sequel, the goal was to keep information secret, closed, and opaque to all those "smelly Walmart" voters who had the audacity not of hope, but to vote for Trump. No more letting witnesses like Corey Lewandowski roast helpless Democrat congressmen on live TV. No more letting Jim Jordan and Matt Gaetz treat dishonest witnesses as piñatas before tens of millions of viewers.

The Democrats' procedures for formulating their charges of impeachment in October 2019 proved to be even more secretive than Ukrainian business dealings and far more secretive, apparently, than the contents of the president's phone calls.

That is not to say that the Schiff playbook to this point was not brilliant and well executed. It was also repugnant to justice. First, Schiff found deep state lifers who really and sincerely believed that they were "the government" and that those of us who won elections were merely the passing fancies of uninformed voters. These people hated Trump and the populist revolution he led. Former ambassadors Bill Taylor and Marie Yovanovitch fit the bill. Department of Defense hack Fiona Hill seemed sent from central casting. She even had the snooty British accent.

Unlike Nadler, Schiff understood the importance of prepared, timed leaks to drive the news cycle. Depositions began at 9:00 AM daily. By 10:00 AM, their carefully crafted opening statement, prepared to put the president in the worst possible light, would be leaked to a media all too willing to play their part in the coup. Stories would be written, narratives furthered, characters developed. They know that stagecraft is statecraft.

By the time Republicans drew blood during a 2:00 PM cross-examination session, the cement of the daily news cycle had already hardened. We had been playing defense, playing catch-up every day, all day. The polls were starting to show it. Days before, I called the president's 2016 deputy campaign manager and overall "MAGA Yoda," David Bossie. David is not a peacetime consigliere. "The *Schiff Show* has been going on eleven days with these closed-door hearings and handcrafted leaks," I lamented. "Be honest. How many of these days have we won?"

"Zerooo!" Bossie exclaimed. "You people are ineffectively defending an innocent president. Get your shit together and do something."

He was right. We had to get Schiff out of the SCIF basement. Only open, aboveground hearings would give us the fair fight we knew we could win. Enough congressional niceties for me. I was busting in to flush the Democrats out—and I'd lead my own coalition of the willing.

Just as Schiff was asking me to leave (again), the SCIF door swung open with force. I didn't see an arm, hand, or face, but a crutch plowing through the opening. Republican Whip and bonafide Ragin' Cajun Rep. Steve Scalise had not long ago been shot by a Bernie Sanders devotee and Southern Poverty Law Center fan and reduced to crutches during his recovery.

"We aren't leaving," he announced. I was relieved to see Steve. I was only partially certain that any of my colleagues would follow me from the routine press conference to undertake the riskier invasion of the SCIF. None disappointed. Leadership can inspire, especially in the spur of the moment. Steve Scalise inspires all who serve among us. It was an honor to have him as my wingman. He stands tall even when he hobbles. Our physical presence, our resistance some might call it, drove home the point in a manner speeches or outraged prose alone couldn't.

The American people were being shut out of the Schiff star chamber, but we had come to jailbreak the truth. Nothing much good happens in basements, and so we wanted sunlight to disinfect the whole process. The media was forced to cover our objections, now made vivid and ripened. Rather than complaining about an unfair process, we had images and video now to show it. And every network ran the video of our operation wall to wall. Perfect. Sometimes you have to put on a show to show up.

To hear critics such as Mieke Eoyang, a former House Intelligence Committee staffer, tell it (in a stream of angry tweets that got reprinted as a Vox article), we had practically raided the Cheyenne Mountain headquarters of NORAD and put the entire apparatus of national security in jeopardy—"a VERY serious national security problem," she tweeted. Spare me.

If anyone violated the great sanctity of the SCIF it was Adam Schiff by turning it into his mysterious kangaroo court. There was no classified information sought or offered during these interviews. Schiff wasn't hiding from the Russians/Chinese/Iranians down in that bunker. He was hiding from us—and we found him.

"You broke the fever!" Steve Bannon's voice and energy are unmistakable. He was the first call I took upon being reunited with my phone. Electronics aren't allowed in the SCIF, even for righteous invaders. Bannon was right. Demonstrative action beats rigid adherence to rules written by others in a game that the people so rarely win. Most Americans would soon agree that the process used by Democrats was unfair. A fall 2019 Politico poll showed only 37 percent of voters supporting impeachment proceedings.

From this, they would never recover. The veil of legitimacy and equity was stripped. This wasn't about Ukraine or Russia or arms—arms that Trump delivered and Obama withheld. The Democrats were being exposed as sore losers. President Trump had promised us that we would win so much that we would get "tired of winning," but every now and again the president needs a great team to help him prevail.

December 9, 2019
House Judiciary Committee.

"You don't get to interrupt me!" I shouted at Stanford Law Professor (and outed "Resistance" member) Pamela Karlan.

When faced with the outrage of others, sometimes it's good to have a reservoir of your own. Never grant the premise of the question, the sanctity of the venue, or the validity of the endeavor to the Left. They were trying to ruin the Trump presidency. Sure, they had contempt for us, but I had more than enough for them. It's not every day that I, a graduate of William & Mary Law School (ranked 31), get to tell a Stanford Law professor (ranked 2) exactly what I think of those who think so little of the American people.

Once we got into a fair fight we had to win it. Then and now, Team Trump doesn't win by playing by the "norms" of Washington aka "establishment rules." Politicians worshipping at the altar of said norms soon find themselves in political graveyards alongside Jeb Bush, John Kerry, John Kasich, and, of course, Hillary. In fact, in each of our most recent presidential contests, the winner seems to have been the candidate who followed the script the least! Don't play by the book if you want to write a chapter of history.

In an era in which everyone has to have a hot take, it's always fun to scald them by reminding them of their worst ones. Karlan was an outraged and outrageous witness. She made fun of the president's minor son's name. On a *Versus Trump* podcast, she revealed how partisan she is by saying, "Conservatives can't even stand to be around each other."

UNC Law Professor Michael Gerhardt, another Democrat impeachment witness, had donated to Barack Obama. Four times.

Harvard Law Professor Noah Feldman was on record writing that Trump should be impeached for mean tweets, owning Mar-a-Lago, and attacking the Fake News. Feldman had previously admitted, also in writing, that impeachment was "primarily, or even exclusively, a tool to weaken President Trump's chances in 2020." Feldman gets some points for honesty there.

These were the "unbiased witnesses" Chairman Nadler called to craft a legal framework for impeachment analysis. Nadler had his own problems, targeted by an AOC-backed primary challenger in his district, and needed to put on an anti-Trump show. A Democratic primary is a dangerous place for an old, unattractive white guy in New York. Just ask now former Rep. Joe Crowley.

BOTH CORRUPTION AND THE RESISTANCE TO AMERICA'S RISING conservative populism should be on plain display for the public, not cooped up in stuffy congressional hearings. I'm sure my aggressive, sometimes angry questioning of these supposed titans of legal education didn't win me votes in faculty lounges. But we aren't governed by them, are we? And they aren't my audience. They were barely my audience when they graded my exams at the William & Mary Law School. Law school "gunners" may one day nestle into cozy tenure and intellectually titillating book clubs. But Firebrands play for the win. The country club can become a funeral home. I wanted the hearings to come alive.

In subsequent hearings, I'd be criticized for attacking Hunter Biden's crack use. Let me be clear. I have nothing against drug addicts or drug users, so long as they don't hurt others. I've known and partied with plenty of both in my wilder days. Hunter admits to wandering around homeless encampments looking for crack, and that doesn't make him a bad guy—though it does make him unlikely to be a legit Eastern European energy savant. Hunter Biden couldn't even resolve a dispute with Hertz Car Rental after leaving his crack pipe, ID, and Secret Service detail's business card in a wrecked vehicle.

That doesn't make him an unsympathetic human. But he probably wasn't leading dispute resolution for Burisma in any competent, non-corrupt way.

July 24, 2019: Conclusion of Mueller Testimony.
Longworth House Office Building. White House operator connects.

"YOU WERE AMAZING. EVERYONE IN THE WHITE HOUSE WAS glued to the TV when you took apart Mueller. Nobody said a word. You kicked his ass!" Trump said.

"Thank you, Mr. President. This bullshit is finally over. Let's get back to making America great again."

"I never stopped," he replied, not knowing what was coming.

The perfect call with the president of Ukraine occurred the next day. And so the coup attempt against Trump revived the day after that. Beria's cynical attitude, as I mentioned above, was "show me the man and I'll show you the crime"—a Soviet mindset that resulted in the prosecutions (over non-Russian matters) of Roger Stone, Paul Manafort, George Papadopoulos, and Rick Gates. Ukraine would then become the more narrowly focused "show me the president and I'll show you the impeachment," no matter how scanty the evidence.

If an investigation requires made-up evidence to proceed, it is a corrupt investigation. With Russia, an FBI lawyer altered emails presented to a secret court in order to spy on Dr. Carter Page. With Ukraine, Rep. Adam Schiff—who once moonlighted as a screenwriter—made up a fake call transcript and theatrically performed it before God and everyone. It was a disgrace to the House—for which Schiff should face ethical sanctions, if Pelosi's House really cares about ethics at all.

The Ukraine controversy teaches us that the establishment is the establishment for a reason. It didn't happen by accident. It happened because they don't take days off, even after a stinging defeat. Their Russia failure didn't deter them from taking the bait on Ukraine. They grind away relentlessly, like the brain-dead zombies they are. It's why it has taken someone with the stamina and magic of Donald J. Trump to beat them over and over again.

Russia and Ukraine were different fights. And we'll have evolving battles ahead to maintain our populist movement. But there is one enemy we always see on the battlefield of ideas: the corrupt media.

They will never stop coming for us, so we must come for them first.

CHAPTER FIVE

ENEMY OF THE PEOPLE

"Let's just stay very focused on impeachment...[and faced with mul-tiple possible interpretations of current events] we shouldn't just pre-tend, oh, this is going one way [or another]. And so all of these moves are toward impeachment."

—JEFF ZUCKER, president of CNN, during a daily 8:00
AM news conference call in 2019 (obtained by guerrilla
journalist group Project Veritas)

THE COMMANDER IN CHIEF KNOWS THAT TO TROLL THE PRESS IS to control the narrative. Flood the zone and the press will drown. He tweets to set the schedule and program the media. This ulti-mately is why they are so angry at his tweets. He doesn't need the press to get the message out, and everyone knows it. It is also why they'll do everything in their power to see that President Trump is muzzled and that never again will another conservative be able to use the latest tech to end-run the press. "This must never happen again," they tell themselves.

For it isn't only politicians or self-important bureaucrats who are threatened by the Trump movement and thus determined to derail it but the professional bloggers-for-billionaires, aka the

#AmericaLast press. Indeed, for all the claims that the media is unfair to the forty-fifth president—they are, and it's worse than you think—it is also undeniable that Trump turns the media into one of his best weapons by feasting on all of the attention he gets, starving his rivals of coverage. Brilliant! To make news, you must break rules and above all be interesting. President Trump is nothing if not interesting. He makes the news because he breaks the news. He doesn't worry the public will be offended by him because he knows that the American people are already mad as hell and aren't going to take it anymore.

As the media get played, while Trump throws the stick and they chase it, their resentment builds. Most media work hand in hand with the most devious #NeverTrump operatives. They share a common objective: destroy, defame, and de-platform powerful "America First" messages and messengers. Their misguided ends justify any means. There are no rules in love, war, or the media. The media companies are rival intelligence networks, paid for by oligarchs who lack even the pretense of due process.

If politics is "Hollywood for ugly people," media is Hollywood for annoying people. The zealot won't change his mind and won't change the topic. CNN's Jeff Zucker knew their mission wasn't just to record events, not anymore. It was to end the Trump presidency. Impeachment or bust!

America deserves leaders bold enough to make history and journalists disciplined enough to report it. Instead, we get the perverted reverse. Politicians witness the events before them as they empower special interests to run government. Media tycoons don't want to make a simple record of that or anything else that transpires. They want to make a *point*. It would probably bore them to be objective.

Jeff Zucker didn't want his journalists to report like neutral witnesses. He wanted them steering events like advocates. Repeat a narrative (or lie) often enough, especially with the appearance of authority and knowledge that TV news anchors possess, and you may make it reality, or at least shape perceptions of whatever events do come to pass. Meme the dream.

You can sense the reluctance with which news operations surrender their grip on a narrative when it bumps up against facts that don't fit their preferred story. Journalists often become angry at both their political foes and the stubborn facts that prove those foes know better than the media.

Witness the scandal—brief yet revealing—over a *Miami Herald* columnist wishing Trump supporters would die from coronavirus.

The thought that some unruly beachgoers might end up having fun during such an important crisis was more than the *Herald*'s Fabiola Santiago could bear, and she tweeted, "[P]acked beaches should work nicely to thin the ranks of Trump/DeSantis/ Gimenez supporters in #Florida who value money over health."

She was soon rightly shamed into deleting the tweet and then brayed a phony non-apology apology, as has become all too common: "I deleted the tweet commenting on people at the beach because it didn't accurately convey my sentiment and I want to apologize for the phrase I used that offended many people. Regardless of political differences, I would never wish any harm on anyone."

Uh-huh. I'm pretty sure that's exactly what she wished.

At least she apologized, but the *Miami Herald* as an institution didn't. They don't feel the need to because, ultimately, they hate those they cover who don't see the world as they do. Sometimes, individual reporters, on rare occasions, have to fall on their swords, but the biased organizations employing them keep on going. Bad as government is, at least when we legislators screw up, we get voted out. Not journalists, unless people get so fed up they stop watching. Then the media company seeks a bailout, as many did during coronavirus. Maybe they should produce a product worth buying?

Even when journalists have to apologize for being a little too blatant in their bias, it doesn't seem to change their subsequent behavior. They aren't really sorry. ABC News analyst Matthew Dowd had to apologize to me in November 2019—after tweeting that the only reason I'm not a "tool" is that "[t]ools are useful"—then had to apologize again to another political figure just two weeks later. He called New York Republican Rep. Elise Stefanik "a perfect example why just electing someone because they are a woman or a millennial doesn't necessarily get you the leaders we need," then deleted the tweet as critics condemned it as sexist.

Dowd later promised to be "better," but I'll believe it when I see it. Be best, as the First Lady says.

The more Americans think of themselves as a single nation, the more the media strategy of pitting groups against each other fails, which, counterintuitively, helps explain their obsession with Russia. Their goal wasn't to unite America against a serious foreign threat, as was the case back in the days of the Cold War. The media's goal, on the contrary, was to convince *some* Americans that *other* Americans weren't really their countrymen, to convince Democrats and moderates that Republicans were dancing on strings pulled by foreign meddlers. Dissent is no longer patriotic if you don't dissent the way we want you to!

The Left claimed that the 2016 election was stolen from Hillary Clinton by a Russian disinformation campaign, but what is the U.S. media if not a massive disinformation campaign itself, one plainly aimed—as Zucker's comments make clear—at certain political outcomes? The irony, of course, is that James O'Keefe, the Project Veritas head who the left-wing media say is not a journalist, makes real news about the fake news. They can't handle it when O'Keefe turns the camera on them.

We accept reporters' official titles, whether bestowed by themselves or the equally self-promoting organizations they work for. But shouldn't some of them be called public relations officers of the Democratic Party?

Take Michael Isikoff, who would prefer you call him Yahoo! News's chief investigative correspondent. Has he really been unearthing buried secrets or is he just an expert mouthpiece for the Democrats' talking points? Is he a stenographer for power or does he hold power to account? Yahoo is barely a search engine, and Isikoff is barely a journalist.

Conservative journalist Sara Carter notes that Isikoff announces events as if they are exciting scoops, but they are more like press releases the Left wants disseminated. Isikoff recently filed an "exclusive" about Obama fretting in a "private" conference call about the "rule of law" being at risk if charges against former Trump national security advisor Mike Flynn are dropped. Do we really think Obama was unaware Isikoff would report on Obama's damning pronouncement? Do we really think Isikoff thought he was exposing Obama's secrets to the world?

Flynn, as noted earlier, was entrapped into uttering minor inaccuracies about Russian contacts, then pleaded guilty to misleading the FBI in exchange for other charges against his son being dropped. The anti-Trump crowd would have us believe they were not personally threatened by Flynn's attempt at reorganizing the intelligence establishment away from its obsession with Russia, but a lot of these people wanted a Cold War with Russia to go on forever because Russia expertise is good for the pocketbooks of the folks in Washington. Chinese is a hard language to learn, man.

The process of stealthily (and sometimes illegally) leaking the establishment's point of view out via superficially objective stories is par for the course in what passes for journalism, but it's less like good reporting and more like a CEO telling his PR flacks what to do. A Democratic politician of Obama's stature can dispense (implicit) marching orders to the journalist-troops as easily and effortlessly as Zucker does to his CNN staff. This politician-media feedback loop is normal for Washington and stretches back to when the press was willing to uphold military secrets or overlook FDR's paraplegia and JFK's philandering.

Journalists ought to be free to make whatever partisan arguments they wish, but it would be illuminating for the public to see just how connected these media figures are behind the scenes, how they happily lap up "leaks" from the Democrats that then lead, in a circular fashion, to stories the same Democrats can point to as evidence that where there's smoke there's fire, which is how the FISA warrants on the Trump campaign/Russia topic were ginned up. It's not a very fun game of telephone when the government can use wiretaps and leaks.

And just as journalists should be free to express their opinions about us, so should we enjoy the right to speak freely about them. After all, a free press doesn't mean a press free from criticism. For an industry built around collecting the scalps of others, they sure seem to have thin skins. It isn't "attacking the press" to demand that it act responsibly.

When President Trump criticizes professional eye-roller and amateurish CNN host Don Lemon for his intellect, Lemon responds by playing the race card. How original. Lemon's CNN colleague Chris Cuomo, upon being confronted as a hypocrite for leaving the house while carrying coronavirus, called the passing citizen who caught him a "fat biker loser."

MSNBC host Joy Reid couldn't explain homophobic posts on her blog, so she blamed hackers without evidence. When even worse comments were found, blaming the U.S. government for conducting the 9/11 attacks, she talked about her subsequent personal growth. I'm glad Joy has grown. But if she were a conservative, she'd be growing off-air. MSNBC awarding her a new nightly show is remarkable only for the double standard it reveals.

Glenn Greenwald writes for the Intercept and other outlets and is no Trump supporter. Indeed he's a socialist and often criticizes the U.S.' supposed imperialism in Latin America. But he sees the way more mainstream media develop a herd mentality, in particular when they go after Trump.

In a May 18, 2020, piece, he praised *New York Times*' media columnist Ben Smith for criticizing another figure usually lauded by the Left, journalist Ronan Farrow ("Is Ronan Farrow Too Good to Be True?"). Smith showed how Farrow's journalistic standards suffered when he went after alleged sexual harassers targeted by the #MeToo movement—that is, when he was concerned with being "good," his work was slightly less likely to be true, or at the very least he didn't strive as hard to verify details.

Smith mentions parallels with Trump's journalist critics in that piece, and Greenwald seconds the observation:

> *What is particularly valuable about Smith's article is its perfect description of a media sickness born of the Trump era that is rapidly corroding journalistic integrity and justifiably destroying trust in news outlets. Smith aptly dubs this pathology "resistance journalism," by which he means that journalists are now not only free but encouraged and incentivized to say or publish anything they want, no matter how reckless and fact-free, provided their target is someone sufficiently disliked in mainstream liberal media venues and/or on social media.*

If the cause is deemed just, in short, you can get away with saying almost anything you want, and the higher-ups aren't going to punish you for it. Sound an off note—something that reveals your reporting is not being done on behalf of the team—and suddenly the media bosses may become very, very skeptical. Smith learned this himself when he published the fake Steele dossier as editor of BuzzFeed. Far from being drummed out of the profession, he was rewarded with a plum position at the *Times*.

Some figures in the media, on CNN in particular, seem to flourish only because they push the correct anti-Trump buttons. How is it possible that figures directly implicated in Trump-era controversies—and possibly in crimes instigated by the prior administration—are now deployed as impartial analysts telling viewers what to make of the latest Trump-related revelations? Are Jim Comey and Peter Strzok the future of the prime-time CNN lineup? It wouldn't be that big a stretch.

Former FBI deputy director Andrew McCabe was found by Inspector General Michael Horowitz to have lied four times, thrice under oath. Shockingly, he has not been indicted. Now he's a CNN paid contributor. "Facts Matter" is a hard mantra to maintain when lies don't matter to hiring.

Former DNI James Clapper lied to Congress about whether the National Security Agency routinely collects information from all Americans' electronic communications, and he resigned upon Trump's election. Today, he is a fixture on CNN, which apparently doesn't worry that this man will lie to viewers. Following the release of Clapper's testimony from the Intelligence Committee, we learned that he told one story on-air to please his CNN overlords and quite another when under oath.

Under Oath Clapper in 2017: "I never saw any direct empirical evidence that the Trump campaign or someone in it was plotting/ conspiring with the Russians to meddle with the election.... I do not recall any instance where I had direct evidence."

CNN Clapper in May 2019: "The Trump campaign was aiding and abetting the Russians!"

Clapper's Obama-era wingman, former CIA director John Brennan, changed his story when he wasn't accountable for lying. "President Trump's Claims of No Collusion Are Hogwash," Brennan wrote for a willfully duped *New York Times*.

But under oath in 2017, Brennan said, "I don't know whether or not such collusion—that's your term—such collusion existed. I don't know.... I don't have sufficient information to make a determination whether or not such cooperation or complicity or collusion was taking place." You didn't see that version of Brennan on TV. It's not what Zucker wanted to hear.

Clapper, Brennan, and McCabe still have paid contributorships. CNN hasn't apologized to their viewers, as they should. But you can't shame the shameless.

Apparently, few things short of ending up in a Miami Beach hotel with a rented male nurse, meth, a disco ball, and erectile dysfunction injections will actually get a pundit kicked off CNN! (Real story—details below!)

The most charitable view of what CNN is doing may be that they simply enjoy having insiders who have access to a great deal of inside information. When Clapper denounced Trump's revoking John Brennan's security clearance and lamented that he wasn't sure if his own was still intact, he may well have been concerned that their commentator gigs would dry up.

Such men are not so much journalists as living, springing leaks, but that's fine with CNN. That's strategically useful intel, for purposes both journalistic and political. You'll be forgiven if you can't tell the difference.

Another figure who keeps getting airtime because he fills an establishment need—unofficial (and of course unelected) spokesman for the military-industrial complex—is neoconservative commentator William Kristol. Kristol teaches us that you don't have to be right to get airtime. He's been wrong on everything for years, from the Iraq War to the motivations and inspirations of today's politics.

Kristol should be completely in his element making political horserace predictions, but he keeps getting those wrong, too—while defending the wrong principles. His clout has diminished so much that when he sent a tweet endorsing Cris Dosev, a 2018 Republican primary opponent for my House seat—and called me "one of the worst GOP members"—not only did Dosev get crushed, he reportedly fretted that Kristol's endorsement would be the kiss of death. I hope he endorses all of my opponents, and for the right price he well may.

Kristol is not the only pundit who makes terrible predictions. Michael Barone predicted Romney would defeat Obama in 2012 by one hundred electoral votes. *New York Times* columnist and Nobel Prize-winning economist Paul Krugman said the internet would have no significant long-term impact on the economy. Dick Morris has been wrong about virtually everything—though back in 2012, he did foretell Trump making good on his long-gestating plans to run for president.

The late Roger Ailes, in his final year at Fox News, recognized that there ought to be consequences for pundits who often err but never doubt. Rupert Murdoch fired Ailes over sexual scandals just as Trump ascended as Republican nominee in the summer of 2016. There are rules about staff, Roger! A year later, Ailes passed away. It would have been fun to watch him wield an axe against all the talking heads who got 2016 so wrong. Ailes was ahead of the rest of Fox News and virtually all the pundit class in recognizing that Trump spoke to the Americans conservatives were trying to reach. "Between the Hudson River and the Sierra Nevada

Mountains, people love Donald Trump," Ailes is portrayed saying in *The Loudest Voice*.

Fox News continues to benefit from the talent choices made by Ailes. Sean Hannity provided the pivotal platform to deliver the facts, winning nightly ratings during the most critical moments of the Trump presidency. Judge Jeanine drove home key themes weekly. Tucker Carlson mocked the absurd claims of the opposition with biting zest. Laura Ingraham set debate panels that were critical to win nightly. Martha MacCallum offered a newsy chance to get information into the bloodstream. Lou Dobbs attacked Republicans who wandered. Each piece was vital to success in its own way.

PRESIDENT TRUMP CALLED THE MEDIA THE "ENEMY OF THE people" one month after taking the oath of office. He set off four years of the media pretending to be afraid that Trump would gut the First Amendment and censor any news he didn't like. Trump didn't have to censor the press to expose their stupidity. He prefers jousting with them to show just how dumb they can be.

Some ought to count themselves lucky they don't get brought up on charges, though, given how deeply enmeshed they are in the possibly criminal political controversies about which they write. They aren't just bystanders. They facilitate the criminality.

When Department of Justice Inspector General Michael Horowitz's report came out in December 2019, the press said it was reasonable for the Obama administration to raise questions about whether Trump associates had inappropriate Russia ties. They ignored the report's conclusion that everything the Obama administration did from that point forward was negligent.

Andrew McCabe and others green-lit an investigation that they knew had little substance, but even more disturbing is the dishonest role the press played in perpetuating that investigation.

McCabe and other deep state operatives would leak items about Trump and his associates, then point to the resulting press reports as "evidence" to justify the continuation of the coup attempt.

Reporters effectively got bribes, too, with their companies paying Democratic oppo research firm Fusion GPS to get Trump dirt, while GPS in turn paid reporters. Since such payments were made from late 2015 to late 2017, this looks like interference with both the election and the then new Trump administration.

Pompous, stick-up-their-ass journos were on the take and on the make for the Democratic Party—albeit indirectly—while they lectured us about corruption. This sort of behavior is not an accident. It isn't just an unconscious bias caused by going to a liberal arts college with mandatory gender identity sensitivity training, or attending too many Resistance rallies. This is conscious, paid-for propaganda. And ultimately, the target isn't Trump. It's you. The media want to mislead you. They really are your enemy, and they are armed and very dangerous.

But if the media hate Trump and an awakened American public, what exactly is it that they love? No matter how rich or powerful the media and their political allies are, they still want to see themselves as champions of equality, as helpers of the "little guy." Narcissism is what powers them.

One weird pattern that emerges, maybe not a very strategically wise one on their part, is that they always try to tear down conservative winners and signal-boost left-wing losers. I say this is strategically unwise because some members of the public start to think that maybe leftists aren't just heroic underdogs. Maybe they deserve their defeat.

This pro-loser strategy, for lack of a better label, gives us phenomena, or pseudo-phenomena, such as politicians Stacey Abrams, Beto O'Rourke, and Andrew Gillum. All darlings of the Left-liberal media apparatus, all talked about endlessly, all complete losers now known mainly for losing but legends in their own minds and in the minds of MSNBC producers.

As I write this in mid-2020, Abrams is credibly talked about as a possible vice presidential running mate for Democrat Joe Biden, though her only real claim to fame is losing a run for Georgia governor, not by the tiny and disputable amount the media likes to imply but by over fifty thousand votes—far too many to be the fault of Republican voter suppression as Abrams likes to claim. Yes, history is replete with efforts to suppress votes, particularly the votes of marginalized Southern blacks. But no one has plausibly alleged that such voter suppression efforts made the difference in that 2018 gubernatorial race. In fact, minority turnout was at a record high in that election. And yet Abrams still lost by a handy margin. But who needs evidence when you can blame your own failures on racism?

It's more like journalists just want to talk about voter suppression and Stacey Abrams in the same segment, then let viewers draw their own (false) conclusions, which maybe will redound to the Democrats' benefit in November 2020. Worth a try, by their low standards. The argument is never made, just slyly implied.

MSNBC's Chuck Todd concluded an interview with Abrams by asking, "Do you worry that no matter *how qualified you are on paper* that the perception that you have not run a large organization as an executive officeholder, or that you have not won state-wide, is a knock against you?"

Qualified on paper? As basically the premise of the question? What?

Stacey Abrams was the minority leader in the Georgia Legislature. As the president might say, I prefer my running mates to be majority leaders. Minority leaders essentially complain for a living. They don't craft policy. I know. I'm in the minority now!

Abrams's answer was head-turning, too. Because she ran a leftist voter registration organization, she claims she was clearly qualified to be number two. Right. Based on FEC filings showing the revenues and expenses of Stacey's make-work job, she'd barely be qualified to own and operate a string of Ruby Tuesdays. Unlike her political hack organization, at least the Ruby Tuesdays would add value—and have killer ribs.

As for Beto O'Rourke, failed Democrat Texas candidate for U.S. Senate from 2018, it was never clear what he stood for that was interesting besides himself—and that wasn't too interesting. Yet the media were happy to say amen to Beto's emptiness. They couldn't get enough of beta male Beto, but it turned out voters could.

Beto understood that eyeballs matter, and he could occasionally be funny or cool (by political standards), but there was no substance there. Beto himself was Beto's only message—and this cult-figure-in-his-own-mind lacked for devoted followers in the real world. The press loved him for some reason. This book will have more substance than Beto's whole campaign, I trust. We are glad to keep Sen. Cruz in the Senate. You can't beat Lion Ted lying down.

Rounding out the most embarrassing media-beloved leftist losers of the 2018 cycle was Florida Man Andrew Gillum. Oh, Andrew. We were told he was the "next Obama" following his failed tenure as Tallahassee mayor. Despite the murder rate in his city rising far faster than the quality of life, he was able to beat three white people for the Democratic nomination for Florida governor. Gillum's fellow African Americans made up about a quarter of the Democratic primary electorate.

Gillum got the media to charge—or falsely imply—that Republican Ron DeSantis was racist. Guilt by association. Quotes out of context. The usual stuff. Gillum lost anyway. But losing wasn't so bad…at first. Gillum got his CNN commentator gig but ultimately traded that for the disco ball and the nurse and the penis injections and all that. If you don't know what I'm referencing, ask Google.

But an arrogant press will continue to push its favorite potential superstars. And it'll hype every disaster that happens on Trump's watch whether it was his fault or not.

The *New York Times* ran the names of a thousand people representing 1 percent of the "nearly 100,000 lives lost to coronavirus," taking up its entire front page, no doubt viewing each death as a rebuke to Trump. One problem—besides Trump having handled the crisis pretty well—is that as soon as rebel journalists started checking the *Times'* list of the dead for themselves, they didn't have to go any farther than the sixth name to find someone who had in fact died not of coronavirus but by being shot. This is your paper of record.

If the *Times* was trying to fan the fires of conspiracy theories about the coronavirus crisis being overblown or a hoax, I guess they accomplished their mission. But I'm sure that wasn't the idea. They pompously introduced the list by saying that the victims were not just "numbers." Fair enough. But some of them also aren't coronavirus victims.

Faced with so much press bias, you can take the "battered spouse syndrome" approach tried by George W. Bush—just hoping one day you'll be able to please your attacker. Or you can be dismissive of the press like Trump, who was asked some gotcha question about oil by a reporter and responded, unfazed, by asking the reporter at what price oil was currently trading. The media have no idea about such real-world details, but they ask the questions they've been told might embarrass the president, which is the important thing.

For good or ill, a free market in journalism means that all the press ultimately cares about are ratings and clicks. Competition exposes losers, and eventually exposes arrogance. In the short term, they'll say whatever promotes the Left, but they're not going to keep saying it if ratings tank and they have to admit they're losing America instead of leading America by the nose, the way they could back in the twentieth century when there were only four big TV networks.

The committed leftists in the media—the ones perfectly happy to let ratings and profits tank if they push the left-wing agenda—may think their principles give them the strength to survive their dwindling ratings, as their core leftist audience ages and eventually dies. But we populists are not *just* free marketeers. We've got a willingness to fight for something bigger than ratings. We'll keep driving home the message of American greatness and pushing back against the elites, both corporate and governmental, even when it means we don't get to be put in heavy rotation on the pundit circuit like the commentators who tell the press what they want to hear.

The establishment is fighting for something very hollow and trying to do it on the sly. We're happy to put on a show and wear our hearts on our sleeves, and one way or another, I think America will get our message. It's a shame we have to fight the media to get that message out.

CHAPTER SIX

MAR-A-LAGO MAGIC

March 9, 2020
Undisclosed location on Palm Beach Island. 5:00 AM...probably.

THERE'S NOTHING LIKE WATCHING THE SUNRISE WHILE KISSING in a hot tub with a Secret Service perimeter protecting you. They're not there, but they're there, if you know what I mean.

Congressman Charlie Wilson didn't have to worry about smartphones or hidden Nest cams during his warm and bubbly rendezvous. It is a rare joy to know with certainty that TMZ isn't hiding in the bushes.

In America, our paparazzi don't take our royalty from us but anoint them—and the Trump family is American political royalty. They are both representative and regal. The Secret Service agents who guard them dig them—and the appreciation and affection are returned.

Mar-a-Lago is a magical place; few other residences have the same aura in the United States. It is a grand palace designed in a different era, yet the glamor, glitz and gold still shine. Especially when the president is on location.

What makes President Trump even more remarkable is that he doesn't surround himself with a cocoon of security or a cadre of aides. This is his home, and one can often see him hopping from table to table during supper. He knows most of the guests and has been friends with some for decades.

Members of the club tend to be very supportive and protective of the president. One such individual, Toni Holt Kramer, started a small group in Palm Beach called the Trumpettes. A socialite group of sophisticated Florida women soon blossomed into an international organization with thousands of members, all to defend and support the president. I love the Trumpettes!

Tiffany Trump always surrounds herself with interesting, pretty people. All the Trumps do. My date for the evening was a stranger the day before. Following an afternoon at the Mar-a-Lago pool, everyone is connected—digitally, politically, socially, and sometimes even familially.

I was in town for a glamorous birthday for the still more glamorous Kimberly Guilfoyle. Along with myself, seated at the head table was the Trump family (gorgeous birthday girl included)—Ivanka, Jared, Eric, Lara, Don, Tiffany, and Michael—along with special guests Tucker Carlson, Anthony Guilfoyle, Sergio Gor—and a good-looking young billionaire who kept hitting on my date. He didn't make the cut for the hot tub later, if you're wondering.

"K. G." is a force of nature in the MAGA movement. Don Jr.'s ride-or-die. The campaign's best fundraiser. A TV superstar. *Una puertorriqueña* with elite America First operative skills. "She's a killer," says POTUS. Don Jr. is lucky to have her by his side. #RelationshipGoals.

"There's my favorite congressman!" Trump exclaimed. "The best. I wish they were all like him. He defends hard. Harder than most. Thank you, Matt. He loves this place."

When I confessed to the president that I liked Mar-a-Lago even more than Camp David, he matter-of-factly replied, "You go for the gold."

The president is happy and gracious when he has friends in his homes and everywhere he goes he is at home even if it doesn't say Trump on the building.

When Donald Trump enters, everyone stands at attention. When he speaks, they learn whom he speaks to. I'm told this was the case at Mar-a-Lago well before his campaign. The clubhouse and beach are breathtaking, sure, but Trump is the main attraction.

My date was radiant like the chandeliers, glowing even, and though totally unaccustomed, she was a quick study. Upon hearing Tucker Carlson humblebrag about his captivating cable show, she said, "It's nice you have a show. What is it about?" Tucker is the best sport. Trump is the star women love even when they don't like him. She was transfixed. Take that, Mr. Billionaire!

She'd later say she's now Tucker's biggest fan. But in these times, who among us doesn't think we are? Tucker recharges by fishing, pondering and debating constantly with friends. It is a blast to be among those to share time with him. We share what we enjoy most.

The party made headlines in various papers. You had to be there to truly experience the magic of celebrating Kimberly's birthday. Dressed in a shiny metallic gold and black dress, while most gentlemen donned tuxedos, toasts were said in her honor. Her best friend and former Fox News producer, Sergio Gor, DJ'd from the music booth above the dance floor. President Trump stopped by the ballroom not once but twice to greet everyone and even sang "Happy Birthday." He brought with him the Brazilian president, Jair Bolsonaro, who had been upstairs having a working dinner earlier that night.

As the beats played, A. J. Catsimatidis and her skintight white dress joined the conga line, while Jesse Watters, with his beautiful wife Emma, sipped champagne by the outside pool. Director of National Intelligence Ric Grenell chatted with Arthur Schwartz over Twitter wars, while Ambassador David Fischer watched in awe as his exuberant wife Jennifer took center stage on the dance floor to Nicki Minaj's "Anaconda." David would go on to heroically coordinate logistics returning Americans home from Morocco during the pandemic. History should note the lives and families he saved.

The night was one to remember, especially after we learned that the Brazilian delegation in attendance was infected with COVID-19. Thankfully, none of us got sick.

As the sun rose the next morning, mimosas and cash flowed. A giant brunch raised millions for the president's reelect from industrialists, moguls, and patriots inspired by his transformational leadership. Unlike Beltway fundraisers, few attendees wanted anything from Trump other than for him to keep fighting! The well-wishing is infectious.

Washington Post reporter David Fahrenthold says no member of Congress has stayed at Mar-a-Lago more than I have. Thanks for noticing, David.

He thinks it's a knock, but then, he isn't invited. Besides, I know it's the best way to serve my country. If you want to be powerful, you have to be proximate. Is a blogger for Jeff Bezos really going to lecture me about the corrosive effects of money in politics? These bloggers-for-billionaires profess to hate the player, the game, and now even the field. If you need help knowing which dates I was there, please use this chapter as a partial guide.

For politics and policy, Mar-a-Lago can't be matched. A translation reinforces the concept of transition itself—"Sea to Lake."

For me it was more "backbencher to presidential counselor," even if only unofficially. Nontraditional settings are indeed my cup of spritzer and where the real work gets done.

The marble busts in the Capitol are great and august (and dead), but no place is bustier than Mar-a-Lago. Plastic surgeon members are happy to point and brag over their tradecraft, funded in part by Florida's arcane and unfair alimony laws. At least in South Florida, as opposed to Washington, the facades hide the slightest insecurity—rather than the soulless corruption. Everyone gets the face they deserve in Florida. Not so in Washington.

President Trump has a unique ability to synthesize information from a bevy of people and stimuli. What other president could build a coalition including Mike Pence and Kanye West? Robert Kraft and Diamond and Silk? Mar-a-Lago is the big, happy, weird intersection of it all. Everyone is having fun and celebrating all the winning, though never for personal benefit—that would be tacky. It's for America!

Trump enjoys seeing other people happy. It recharges him. It's why the rallies matter so much to him. At the club he can let loose a little. Once he even danced in a sombrero for an acquaintance's wedding. But he never stops working on matters large and small. And in the contest for the president's policy indulgence, you must be present to win.

January 2, 2020
Mar-a-Lago. Main dining promenade.

"Come over here. Pull up a chair. I didn't know you were here."

"Your daughter Tiffany invited me, sir."

Enough pleasantries. I had to make my argument while POTUS was chewing his meat loaf. Otherwise, he was talking. I had to give him something else to chew on.

"Mr. President, Tucker Carlson and I had to stop us from going to war with Iran once before—when they downed that drone. Are we going to have to do it again?"

I had interrupted Kevin McCarthy's one-on-one dinner with the president. Kevin didn't love the third wheel. I didn't care. Besides, I was about to go on Shannon Bream's Fox News show and would be among the first to frame the U.S. air strikes killing Iranian Quds Force General Qasem Soleimani. When Trump knows you're going on TV he's eager to advise and banter. Stage-craft is statecraft. President Trump and I respect the airtime.

The president immediately got Tucker on the phone.

"I'm with Gaetz."

(Inaudible response.)

"No, he's not with a woman."

(Inaudible response.)

"I know, he's an animal."

The talk of war and peace and women continued as the vanilla ice cream was devoured. Two scoops, please. The president made the right call—kill Soleimani to avoid a war, not start one. He reset deterrence, defined the exquisite reach of U.S. lethality, and made thousands of Americans safer in the Middle East and elsewhere. At Mar-a-Lago, he could get perspectives beyond the Beltway. I'm honored to help curate just a few.

"Write that down! Give me three paragraphs." President Trump will regularly assign snap written exams to his advisors when discussing ideas. He knows a sizzling rhetorical approach or phrase can win the day. He is a master brander. I've scratched out some of my best prose under pressure at the Resolute Desk, on Air Force One, and riding in the Beast, as the armored presidential limo is known. But hearing the president share a strong ambition for peace, not more war, I was eager to help him. My scribblings on a Mar-a-Lago cocktail napkin calling for Iran to accept peace remain among my proudest contributions to my country.

January 1, 2020
9:00 PM, Mar-a-Lago off-site security checkpoint.

"SIR, THERE APPEARS TO BE SOMETHING METAL IN YOUR BACK pocket. Do you mind checking it again?"

The wand kept beeping. I was annoyed, tired, and frustrated. And then terribly embarrassed.

New Year's Eve had not gone well. I had invited a date I adored to Key West to enjoy a celebration with two of my best friends—Dr. Jason Pirozzolo and Savara Hastings, who own a home together in the Conch Republic. The dancing was fun, the music the best. Apparently, the adoration went only one way. Not even a ball-drop kiss. Expectations were unfulfilled to say the least. Can't win 'em all.

Alone and romantically crestfallen on a Key West beach, I got a call from Tiffany Trump. "Why aren't you here at Mar-a-Lago? Michael and I adopted kittens and they want to meet you." Tiffany and her fantastic boyfriend Michael know I'm a sucker for animals and dearly miss having them while serving in Congress. Mar-a-Lago and kittens were just the pick-me-up I needed. I started driving.

Members of Congress get waved into the Capitol and White House without the hassle of metal detectors or scanners. Not so at the Winter White House. When I realized what I had pulled out of my back pocket, I could feel the humiliation wash over me like an intense wave of Florida humidity.

"Cover your stinger!" read the foil wrapper of the condom I had acquired in the Key West Airport. The smiling yellow and black flying insect pictured was taunting me. He wouldn't be so happy if he had spent the night bickering with my date at Irish Kevin's.

I still wince whenever I hear my Secret Service unofficial code name—"Bumble Bee."

Float like a butterfly, sting like a bee, indeed.

CHAPTER SEVEN

TWO PARTIES, ONE SCAM

December 22, 2018
The White House. Private residence. Government shutdown strategy lunch.

"MR. PRESIDENT, IF YOU'D LIKE, I CAN THUMBNAIL THIS FOR YOU."

Vice President Pence understands how Washington works, having risen in the ranks in the House of Representatives before becoming Indiana's governor. He always strives to provide helpful insight. It was time to cut a deal with Sen. Schumer and the Democrats and end the shutdown, he reasoned. We needed a bipartisan deal. We needed the deal more than we needed the wall, political asylum reform, or internal enforcement of immigration laws at scale. Other smart establishment thinkers were quick to agree, and ultimately, so did President Trump. The president's decision weeks later to end the shutdown without every dime of border security money he rightly requested was one of the very few dips in his historically durable approval rating.

For populist conservatives, the frustration is that the energy that drives our movement doesn't always convert into the bold policy decisions American greatness demands.

It wasn't supposed to go this way. Immigration hard-liners Reps. Mark Meadows, Jim Jordan, Andy Biggs, and I had gone to the White House to convince the president to hold firm and hold out if necessary. After all, we felt border security was an essential function of government that has been ignored by both parties for far too long. Nobody was chanting "Build the bipartisan consensus!" at any MAGA rally I've attended. Maybe that is because the Trump movement is energized by the need to make things different and better—not keep them the same. President Trump is a Firebrand because he is so rarely satisfied with anything short of America's best. Bipartisanship is too often the opposite of reform or improvement.

Comedian George Carlin said, "The word 'bipartisan' usually means some larger-than-usual deception is being carried out." I'm sure that was true in Carlin's heyday, though now bipartisanship is the all-too-usual mechanism of deception—the standard way of selling out the country to fuel the largesse of Washington and the greed of its managers. The special interests love a system that demands bipartisanship to get things done. That way, exploitation looks like peaceful coexistence and real change looks like inappropriate partisanship. As the Senate functions today, just one person can have significant ability to block meaningful legislation. It is the tyranny of the minority and D.C. loves it—because the real majority outside of Washington doesn't like the politicians and gets even more suspicious when a handful of them appear to be gumming up the works of the government's usual functioning. That's an unfortunate misconception on the public's part because much of business as usual in Washington is highly destructive.

The greatest opportunity we have as Americans to fight back against the corrupt uniparty is the Trump presidency. Candidate Trump had little reverence for how things had been done before. When Trump was booed at debates, he made a point to call out the lobbyists and establishment hacks who fill the debate halls. Trump will never be part of the uniparty because he may be the first American politician to successfully run against it as a foil. Trump campaign strategist Steve Bannon put it succinctly: "We made Hillary Clinton the defender of the corrupt status quo." Stagecraft is statecraft.

President Trump wasn't just attacking the uniparty power brokers on the Left—he pushes back on his own administration's dogmas more than any president in American history. We have a champion and an opportunity here, though overcoming the power structure of D.C. means facing strong headwinds.

There are strong bipartisan majorities in favor of accumulating national debt, creating new entitlements, irresponsibly printing money, bowing to Big Tech, invading faraway lands, and importing cheap illegal labor. Bipartisanship gave us trade deals that sold out American workers for multinational corporations and a limp-wristed China policy. It allowed our higher education institutions to trick teenagers into accepting a life of indebtedness for worthless degrees. The worst things our government has done to our own people have been delivered through unholy cooperation. This is the agenda of the uniparty, and it must be stopped.

Both parties have an interest in keeping things almost exactly as they are. Sure, they'll try to press an advantage against the other side, maybe catch the wave of a big popular cause sweeping the nation once in a while. But for the most part, they fear that a true political upheaval could disrupt their luncheons, campaign donations, speaking schedules, and staffing needs. They've got it pretty good. Why risk messing that up?

The inertia of Permanent Washington doesn't uniquely benefit Republicans or Democrats in a zero-sum game against one another. It benefits most those corruptible officials willing to work across party lines to screw all Americans.

Keep rubber-stamping those continuing budget resolutions and voting with your party on the big votes, then writing triumphant—or angrily defeated—press releases about it to the folks back home, as if you really worked up a sweat about it all, and the odds are you can stay here for years. You won't need to change and grow, and the government won't change much, either, though it will gradually grow, like an obese person without the will to change their eating habits.

If coasting like this means not daring to make any big changes in a country that badly needs them, well, that's a shame, but first things first, and each member can tell himself, "It's not my fault." There are 535 of us here, and I do what I can, sometimes. It'd be nice if the whole system got fixed, if each member thinks at one time or another, but since that's unlikely to happen, I should just keep working the system to my own advantage. It wasn't easy to devise a system where nobody is responsible for failure and managed decline is a regular Tuesday, but they did it.

To maximize the odds of Congress working for you—to get both parties to cut spending, chop away at red tape, tackle the debt—we will have to replace the quiet but immense scam the two-party aristocracy has perpetuated with a populist sense of urgency and non-crony priorities. That will have to mean some turnover in Congress, I'm sure. It also means working with the populists on the Left when it suits us strategically, even if we know they want to turn America into a dystopian Woketopia.

I've sponsored legislation with Bernie Sanders's national campaign cochairman Rep. Ro Khanna to stand against Middle East wars. AOC and I have taken on the drug companies to research and democratize access to marijuana, MDMA, and psilocybin for veterans. Rep. Zoe Lofgren of California and I work together to stop warrantless government spying on Americans. This is a more productive, populist bipartisanship to take on the establishment of both parties!

The 116th Congress has some heroes and fighters in it, but the establishment is people as well as an almost perpetual mindset. We'll need more populists, more people in both parties who are frankly disgusted by what Washington has become and thus motivated to do things differently.

For now, I think only the Republican Party—and we're lucky if we even win over that party—is going to rise to the challenge. But if there is to be a bipartisan consensus in the future, a time after the fierce and necessary fighting ahead, let that consensus be a populist one, not an exploitative elite one. Let future congresses be filled with people committed to reducing the level of nonsense in Washington, not swamp creatures who pride themselves on being seen at the annual Gridiron Dinner.

The establishment won't roll over or disappear just because a few of us tell it to get lost, but if we are persistent—and the establishment, by its very nature, remains lazy and unimaginative— we populists might at least be able to lead here. A vocal enough minority can make a big difference, and if the parties we have don't offer voters real choices and real differences, our vocal populist minority will have to behave like a party unto itself.

I think it's the unofficial new party America will end up supporting. They've been duped by the other two for far too long.

June 18, 2019
Air Force One. Presidential Office. Traveling to Orlando
for Trump 2020 campaign launch.

"IT'S GOING TO BE HARDER FOR THEM TO IMPEACH ME NOW THAT I've announced for reelection, right?"

I replied, "No, it isn't. They're still going to impeach you. They can't help themselves. We will make them pay for it, sir, I promise. And the people will return you to the White House to keep winning."

My response wasn't as uplifting as I had hoped. The president half shrugged and returned to the final edits of his speech. He didn't want to be impeached. "It's not good for the resume," he would half joke.

Impeachment may very well be the best thing that ever happened to President Trump, though. He faced their toughest political weapon and withstood it resiliently. All Democrats and even some Republicans indulged it. Bipartisanship at its worst, at least until we got the rest of the Republicans properly aligned and some healthy fighting between the two parties started. In a second term, to solve America's major challenges, President Trump will have to take on the establishment in both parties again. He will have to prioritize immigration reform and trade. He's just the leader to do it. The uniparty is on notice.

CHAPTER EIGHT

ENDING ENDLESS WARS

January 10, 2020
Arlington Cemetery. Funeral of SFC Mike Goble. 7th SFG. U.S. Army.

"Do what you can to bring them home, Matt."

The fallen hero's godfather had long hair and a beard. Neither had seen a brush in a while. He had more important things to do. If he didn't have time for a pressed shirt, he surely didn't care to use protocols, titles, or last names. "Matt" was fine by me. We don't put on airs when we put our people in the ground.

A tear-drenched godmother showed me a wrinkled photo of my fallen constituent proudly waving a Trump flag with one arm and hugging his military brothers with the other. "Tell the president Mike loved him."

"Sir, the president has been trying to reach you." My outstanding military aide Charles Truxal knew why, as did I. He handed me the phone as we walked out, past the flag-draped casket. I always cry at military funerals. Sometimes I ugly cry. I wish I didn't. It is weakness in the presence of strength. But a great country should shed tears for those who shed blood for her. We should feel the pain of every life lost and carry it with us as long as we live, especially when we carry the weight of the decision to send them there. The dead die twice when we forget them and what they lived for. There is something so painful about losing one of our best in the middle of his service to country. A life cut down before it could grow full. So many other lives changed forever.

President Trump wanted me to vote against legislation I helped draft that would limit his ability to begin an extended war against Iran. No president has been more anti-war in my lifetime than Donald Trump. Still, no president, including Trump, should be able to draw our people into endless, unfocused, undisciplined, unconstitutional wars—especially in the sands of the Middle East, which have been soaked in too much proud, patriotic, American blood. Castles in the sand and democracies in the sky can never be built. Self-government means self-sacrifice. We can't do it for others any more than they can do it for us.

It's hard when you disappoint your heroes—but my hero was in that casket.

"Mr. President, I just buried one of my constituents. He was a big fan of yours. I promised his family I'd tell you. They know we talk. His daughter is six years old."

The commander in chief is also the consoler in chief. "Tell them I'm doing all I can to end these wars. I'm more anti-war than you are, Matt. I believe what you believe even more than you believe it. Promise me you'll tell them." I carried the message to America's newest Gold Star family, my voice cracking as I relayed our president's gratitude.

"I don't want you to do this. You're hurting my leverage, but I know you feel it in your heart. I'm not going to bust your balls over this." We've never discussed that vote again—at least not directly.

LATER THE PRESIDENT WOULD TWEET, OSTENSIBLY TO ALL MEM-
bers of Congress, to "vote your heart." I'm not the first man to get
a love note tweeted by our president—that honor would fall to my
fellow millennial Kim Jong-un—but I sure took it that way.

Along with the president, my heart breaks when the blood
of America's bravest patriots is wasted unwisely by men who
then turn around and pretend that they did nothing wrong as
they cash in.

Former Secretary of State Colin Powell endorsed Joe Biden
for president—just as he had the warmongers Barack Obama and
Hillary Clinton. Hey, I wonder how the Iraqis feel about him
supporting a candidate who called for breaking Iraq into three
countries?

Powell warned that if you break it, you bought it. But he and
Biden were among the breakers. We are still paying the price, with
rising costs in dollars and lives. Real courage isn't backing a man
who Obama's own secretary of defense, Robert Gates, said was
"wrong on nearly every major foreign policy and national security
issue over the past four decades."

CNN breathlessly pretended that Powell's endorsement was
some courageous breaking of political ranks. Powell was the front
man for bad intelligence. He should wear that for the rest of
his life.

Indeed, the last time I listened intently to Colin Powell, it
was eighteen years ago, and he was saying something ominous
about WMDs in Iraq. Unfortunately, others were listening, too.
Not so much with Donald J. Trump, who called bullshit and later
called George W. Bush a war criminal to a standing ovation in
South Carolina—one of our most pro-military states. That was
the moment that I knew everything would be different. Because
everything about it was true. Finally.

Courage requires truth-telling. Powell couldn't tell the truth to the nation, the world, or even President Bush and Shadow-President Cheney. I doubt he can even tell the truth to himself. I wonder if he even knows it now. We don't get to use truth serum on network news, though everyone would tune in. I told Trump the truth about my vote when we disagreed. I wouldn't authorize a blank check for another generation of neocon desert adventures at the expense of America's finest and bravest.

This is not a policy debate. The victims of bad military decisions are my neighbors. We play cornhole at KC's Sandbar & Grille in my hometown of Fort Walton Beach. I know what they signed up for because they tell me why they signed up for it. I know they'd die for America as often as God would allow. For some, it is a family endeavor—parents hand off the family commitment to daughters and sons. For others, it is a private, almost spiritual commitment to the country they love.

They will never run from a fight, but we have a responsibility to make sure it is winnable and worth winning. Fake leaders have no license to spend their lives frivolously, as Powell, Biden, and Cheney have. Capt. Nathan Hale regretted that he had but one life to give for his country. My people give their all—their arms and legs, their backs, and scrambled minds. They give their youth, their marriages, their everything. They carry that service with them in the boardroom and in their kids' bedrooms as they tell the stories, but they never leave it behind. Those who don't come home alive—and we never leave them behind even when they are not breathing—hang around in the minds of their moms, dads, and kids, who soldier on without their soldiers long after the medals are doled out and the obits are written. Great Americans always carry on. Military families inspire the best within us because they are the best among us. They'll go to any land we ask, even to space, because we ask.

My baseball coaches wore pilot bags. My scout leaders were air commandos. My Baptist deacon maintains the flight line. My amazing Chief of Staff Jillian Lane-Wyant is a marine spouse. During Florida's legislative session, a bomb technician fed my cat.

I will never send America's troops, our neighbors, into a fair fight. Rather, I intend on providing the funding, equipment, infrastructure, and arms to achieve decisive victory every single time. We build the best weapons ever because we, and we alone, never hope to fire them. We trust our best.

A well-funded force need not be so well worn. Today our military is overstretched, over-deployed, and overexerted. Growing up where I have, I've seen my whole life what endless deployments and unfocused wars truly mean for our best people: tearful airport goodbyes. Bargaining with God for the safe return of loved ones. Parenting disrupted. Marriages destroyed. Extra psychiatrists at our schools. Drug abuse. Domestic violence. Veteran suicide. Shattered limbs, broken hearts, and grieving families at Walter Reed Hospital. Caskets draped in flags. Gold Star families in mourning. Roads, parks, and schools named in permanent reverence for the fallen.

The "fog of war" is no fog to me, nor to any of the seven hundred thousand people I serve. It is weird to talk about service when so many of my constituents serve me and indeed all of us. I never wore the uniform, but I never go long without seeing it profoundly displayed.

We see the impact of war every day on the people we love who shape our lives. It starkly reminds us that the unmatched freedoms we enjoy are not free—they are bought with the blood of American patriots. And it is our solemn duty and highest responsibility to make sure that this sacred currency is spent only when absolutely necessary. Unfortunately, our decision-makers have fallen short of this standard, as they have with most standards. They demonstrate a tragic recklessness.

Of everyone in Congress, I represent the highest concentration of active-duty military. In my district, nobody is too woke to stand for our anthem—even if some stand on prosthetics. We don't kneel except in prayer, though we do a lot of that here, too.

Under the America First banner, a new generation of Republicans must stand against endless unfocused unconstitutional wars. We are not isolationist when we call for intelligent exercise of military power. The Bush-Cheney-Clinton-Haley-Cheney desire to start three new wars before lunchtime tomorrow is the undisciplined behavior of an unserious nation in decline. My soldiers, sailors, and airmen deserve better leaders than they've gotten. They'll have to make do with me while I try to do right by them.

There are times when the fight is just and necessary. But it isn't naive—as the self-appointed experts would tell us—to rebuild America's crumbling infrastructure before we rebuild Kandahar (sometimes for savages who, even when fighting on our side, rape young boys in their tents as we shrug, and then they frag us). Whereveristan should never come before Main Street, USA.

America First means nation-building at home and an admission that we are not the world's police force or piggy bank. We should secure every inch of the U.S. border with Mexico (and maybe even Canada) before we send the first American patriot or dollar to defend Saudi Arabia's border with Yemen, Syria's border with Turkey, or Iraq's border with Iran. How can a nation unserious about its own border spill trillions defending borders and Bedouins oceans away and eons away from our level of civilization? It would be like your neighbor criticizing your marriage while he sleeps with the babysitter.

We have spent $6 trillion in Iraq and Afghanistan—a staggering sum. That is more than the market cap of Facebook, Apple,

Google, and Microsoft combined. Plus our entire nation's credit card debt and student loan debt combined. We've indebted our own people while pouring money into the hands of some who have hated us for hundreds of years and will probably still hate us for hundreds more. They have long memories in the Middle East. We have long accounts receivable notes that will only convert to regrettable debt.

Despite the loss of American lives and treasure, I don't know that we can honestly claim that our efforts have deprived terrorists of the means and the land to plan future attacks. Today, the Afghan government is divided in chaos and in corruption—just as it always was and may always be. We spent nineteen years trading the same villages back and forth with the Taliban. The *Washington Post*'s Afghan Papers proved that we never knew what we were doing, and we let warfighting heroes die as their clueless leaders in the Pentagon, and the Bush/Obama White Houses, continued to believe that fortitude over function could deliver victory which we couldn't define, much less achieve.

Treasonous bullshit, if you ask me, to keep letting Americans die because armchair retired generals needed paying contracts and defense contractors needed stock dividends.

Strong borders. Energy dominance. Building a resilient homeland and bringing investment back to our country. These things do more for our national interest than ill-fated interventionist regime-change wars. As President Trump reminds us, economic security is national security. It means better trade deals, a strong manufacturing base, and capital investment returning from foreign bank accounts to invest in our people. Personnel is policy, and our policy has been to neglect training up our personnel. We have also failed to let people keep what they earn. Let them be rewarded, and allow the creativity of our great nation to lead the world. Bush's military "coalition of the willing" wasn't leadership. It didn't inspire our allies. It was more like dragging people on a forced visit to your in-laws…if they lived in a cave in Afghanistan!

I'm grateful that President Trump is the first president since Ronald Reagan who has not started a new, extended war. He has functionally ended our involvement in the Syrian Civil War, and almost every time we talk he is trying to bring more home.

Securing the homeland does not require America to invade every nation where terrorists huddle, and it certainly does not require staying there and becoming the Neighborhood Watch program. President Trump knows how to deal with bullies. You punch them in the face and give them a reason to think twice before messing with you again. You don't move into the bully's home for twenty years in a quixotic effort to have them unlearn their wicked ways. Forty-six missiles landing on a Syrian airbase, launched from far away, sends a message—to Iran, Russia, and China. Killing Iranian military leader Soleimani with a drone guided from the homeland resets deterrence. Decades clinging to the frozen mountains of the Hindu Kush, by contrast, have been exhausting. What would winning look like if we won there anyway? An Afghanistan stable enough for multinational corporations to export our jobs to?

I am proud to stand for our troops, our flag, and our national anthem—and this son of Northwest Florida is equally proud to stand against stupid wars managed by stupid men, and Hillary.

One would think the cautionary tales of Afghanistan and Iraq would make the war lobby and so-called "national security experts" more cautious about U.S. involvement. Instead, Hillary Clinton, with the support of hawks in the Republican Party, launched a regime-change operation in Libya, removing the strongman dictator Qaddafi.

More recently, my Republican colleague Rep. Liz Cheney of Wyoming has picked up the neoconservative pantsuit Hillary

Clinton left behind, in contrast to the more effective, realistic Trump Doctrine. Liz has supported ten of the last three wars. When President Trump correctly removed tens of Americans from the Turkey/Syria border, Liz was among his loudest critics. She joined with a majority of House Republicans in rebuking the Trump Doctrine in Syria. Have the lives of Americans suffered because our troops aren't as involved as Liz would like in Syria? Did she want a new war with Turkey, an on-paper ally? As I said on the floor of the House in October 2019:

If Turkey is not acting like a NATO ally, perhaps the sensible solution is to remove Turkey from NATO rather than keeping the United States inserted in Syria, presumably forever.... I've heard my colleagues say we should not leave Syria without a strategy. Perhaps it is equally logical that we should not stay in Syria without a strategy.... In Syria, we have tens of Americans stuck between armies of tens of thousands who have been fighting for hundreds of years and will likely be fighting hundreds of years from now. Our mission, to deprive ISIS of Caliphate land, has largely been accomplished—with the help of the Kurds and with over $9 billion being paid to the Kurds. The Kurds have been fighting bravely where they live.... They have been trained, funded, and equipped by the United States.... We cannot accept the proposition that if we support a group of people because our interests align in one case, this somehow morally binds our country to every conflict they have—past, present, or future. To do this would constrain the utility of America's future alliances, not strengthen them.

"We have to fight them over there so we don't fight them over here," the neocon chant goes. Even if you insist that this rule is true in the Middle East, I think we can all agree that it doesn't apply to Germany. Well, maybe not all of us.

When President Trump announced the withdrawal of one-third of U.S. troops from Germany in June 2020, Liz Cheney called the president "dangerously misguided." We had "abandoned allies" and "retreated" from the "cause of freedom" itself, she tweeted. In Germany?!

A Cheney supporting the Cheney Doctrine over the Trump Doctrine isn't surprising. Liz wants Trump to lose, hoping that a reset of republicanism will quell the unruly populists and reempower the establishment. We were elected together and entered Congress together. On one of our first meetings, Rep. Cathy McMorris Rodgers had purchased each new Republican member a "Make America Great Again" hat for an inaugural "class photo." Liz was the only incoming GOP member who refused to don the hat and join the rest of us. Abandoning allies indeed.

Most recently, Rep. Cheney has teamed up with Democrat Rep. Jason Crowe to draft and introduce legislative barriers to a Trump-led Afghanistan troop drawdown. They want to stay forever.

Many in Washington can think of literally no place in the world they wouldn't want more troops, more spending, and more problems to justify more troops and more spending. If we are so scared that Russia is going to roll tanks through Germany, why isn't Germany scared enough to stop buying Russian oil? On military spending, we have been the fool of the world for too long, and we have been played accordingly. Trump doesn't tolerate it. He sees that it is grotesque, particularly when the pro-war forces place the veneer of freedom and humanitarianism over their lust for power.

There is nothing humanitarian about the slave markets thriving in Libya, or the migrant crisis wreaking havoc across Europe. We had a deal with Qaddafi. He turned over his nukes and we turned over a new leaf in our relationship with his country—that is, until the Clinton-Boltonistas decided that they needed to look tough or something (it was never quite explained). So much for the Libya model! On to the next one! There should be a rule that neocons must live in the countries they invade—not just rape the government contracting process on the rebuilding of the country, as they did in Iraq.

The same "thought leaders"—or is it trend followers?—were equally desperate for regime change in Syria and the removal of Bashar al-Assad. Like Qaddafi, there was no question he was a brutal dictator. The problem with the misguided calls for regime change is the lack of a credible, superior alternative to the dictator—the main beneficiaries of such an intervention in Syria would be ISIS and the related terrorist groups fighting Assad and benefiting from chaos.

Luckily, the forever war lobby never got its desired intervention in Syria, largely thanks to Donald Trump—the only major presidential candidate who spoke against the folly. The so-called "experts" behind our failed foreign policies have not learned from their mistakes because they have never been asked to explain them or even acknowledge them. And so today the saber-rattling persists, with bigger, brighter bombs and bombast, and is directed now toward Venezuela, Yemen, and, most disturbingly, Iran.

As we look to these countries, it is our task to ensure that we don't just repeat the mistakes of yesteryear's decision-makers but that we learn from them. We must resolve not to start unwise wars or place our military in unwinnable and endless conflicts. We know from tragic experience that oppressors like Maduro, Rouhani, and even Kim Jong-un will use military conflict with the United States as a scapegoat for their own considerable failures, then export violence and undermine the organic desire of their people to seek freedom.

In Yemen, Syria, Libya, and beyond, we shouldn't fool ourselves into thinking that unwilling or unreliable local fighters necessitate the involvement of American troops. The examples of Afghanistan, Iraq, and Libya—just to name a few—teach us that it is wrong to presume that just beyond the lifespan of every dictator lies a peaceful, Jeffersonian democracy, rather than generations of anarchy, violence, terrorism, and chaos. Things can and frequently do get worse. The number of failed states is growing, not declining, and we cannot stop that number's growth any more than we can stop the tides from coming in or hurricanes from making land-fall. We must endure them and see to it that their misery doesn't become our misery. This is achievable absent multi-decade land wars and occupations.

If our enemies mistook a more precise American focus as a disengaged, disinterested, or recoiled America—an "isolationist" America—and tested our resolve or capability by attacking us, they would find us recoiled like a viper: ready to strike instantly, lethally. Military action, including intervention, is always on the table—but only as a last resort, and only when there is a direct, concrete, and grave threat to the security of the United States or to one of our allies. Just as the threat must be clear, concrete, and well defined, so must be the objectives of military operations. We must know what victory looks like in order to achieve it. It must be seen first in the mind before it can be won on the field of battle.

Freedom is the most precious thing in the world—and it is for that very reason that freedom must be fought for and won by those who yearn to live it most. Freedom cannot be America's gift to the world, purchased with the blood of U.S. service members alone. Nothing given has value, only that which is earned.

The neocons believe freedom can be bought on the cheap, and in so thinking they take too low a view of what makes us great. For oppressed people to live any lasting liberty, they must make it happen themselves. They must fight and die for it, bury their relatives over it, and tell timeless stories of national heroes who showed the bravery to win. They must teach their children that it matters and that there is nowhere to run should they fail. Only then will any people cherish freedom so much that they will not allow a strongman to take it away ever again. It is true that some of them will die, but they'll have something worth living for. This attitude is less likely to produce gratuitous, pointless military deployments than would aimless, global patrolling and policing operations.

Plenty of D.C. pundits and Beltway hawks talk in terms of "toughness" to support American military action. They say America has a "moral obligation" to intervene everywhere. Real morality and real toughness is standing up to the pro-war special interests, who never tire of tiring out America. Real morality is affirming forever that the blood of American troops is not for sale, not at any price, not at any time.

Today's wiser, more cautious Trump Doctrine will rile some so-called "experts" in Washington, but it is supported by an over-whelming share of Americans. And President Trump's measured approach in Venezuela, Syria, and Iran will make our nation stronger. We must continue to build upon Trump's achievements in developing a twenty-first-century foreign policy. Elected office-holders of both parties have sworn an oath to uphold and defend the Constitution, which requires specific declarations of war from Congress, not just endless enemy hunting. Will the members of Congress keep their oath?

This means not sending the next generation of patriots to fight unwinnable wars, for unknowable gain. There are always places we could invade, peoples we could rescue, nations we could build. A clear-eyed look at the threats we face proves that peace through strength should also mean strength through peace.

Our doctrine means continuing to rebuild our military and maintaining its dominance and hegemony. It means listening to the American people, not the siren song of beltway pundits and armchair generals in fancy air-conditioned studios. It means taking a clear-eyed look at America's interests, always focusing on the well-being of our own great nation before we volunteer our brave soldiers to the world. It means knowing that, sometimes, the fight is just, and worth fighting—and knowing that when America fights, America will win and win quickly. A great people don't make the next generation go to war to settle scores from the last. We cannot send Generation Z to die in Afghanistan. Our heroic servicemen deserve better, and the enduring prosperity of our nation depends on it.

If we must fight some nation purely because of its size and potential hostility, let's get to the fight that really matters—China. But that doesn't mean mindlessly launching missiles. We must be smarter to win the fights that matter most.

February 10, 2020
4:00 PM, Air Force One. Manifested to Manchester, New Hampshire, for "Make America Great Again" rally.

THE LOUDSPEAKER VOICE WAS FAMILIAR BY NOW: "THE PRESIdent has boarded the aircraft." The commander in chief then bounded to the conference room where his political team gathered.

"The soldiers are at Dover [New Hampshire]. We should go to Dover. Does anybody mind if we cut the rally short and head back to make it?" No time was permitted for a response. He had already made the call and given the order. "We are going to Dover." He returned to his office not having heard a word from the rest of us. The manifest was updated to Dover.

They weren't just any fallen heroes. They were mine. The 7th Special Forces Group calls my district home. They go deep into the fight and take heavy casualties. I've buried too many. They were all in their prime. The last two were twenty-eight years old.

9:45 PM, Dover Air Force Base. Dignified transfer of Sgt. Javier "Jaguar" Gutierrez and Sgt. Antonio Rodriguez.

"WE HAVE TO DO THIS TO SHOW EVERYONE THE COST OF THESE wars, Matt," said President Trump. We hadn't stepped off Air

Force One yet. The tears were already welling in my eyes. Did I mention I cry?

I can still hear her screams. I will never forget them. Spanish words, raw emotions. *"Estoy aquí, Jaguar! Estoy aquí!"* She didn't believe he was dead and was shouting, "I'm here." She sprinted to the back of the C-130, calling for him at the top of her lungs. When she saw the casket, knees buckled, hearts sank, and reality set in. It was the hardest thing I've ever had to watch in my life.

Vice President Pence handed each and every family member a card, saying, "If you need anything large or small, you call this number. We will help you."

As we loaded back onto the presidential aircraft, Sen. Rand Paul of Kentucky said of Trump, "He's exactly where we are, Matt. We have to keep helping him. And them."

And I will.

CHAPTER NINE

CHINA IS NOT OUR FRIEND

THERE IS A STORY WE TELL OURSELVES THAT CHINA WILL BEHAVE just like us. We just need to invite them in, show them more of the Western world, bring them closer. This is a lie. Exposing the truth will help us see China—and our leaders who indulge them—clearly.

When we think of great power politics, we often obscure it in the niceties and sophistries of diplomacy. Gentle words smooth over the harsh reality of Swiss bank accounts and Panama Papers bribe records. It's easy to talk abstractly, hard to have a real talk. But there is a kind of power that comes with telling the truth, a natural hierarchy that separates who is serious from who is seriously wrong, sometimes identifying good and branding evil. It just so happens Donald Trump is the best brander in the world.

Our first obligation is to tell the truth about China without the clutter of old trade deals and riches that never quite materialized (except for the elites, of course). To be candid, we must know who we are and who they are. We must be as aware of our own weakness as they are of ours. After all, they've had centuries of reading *The Art of War* and we have a president who has written *The Art of the Deal*. President Trump knows when to use sticks and carrots to get a negotiation moving. But the time may have passed for carrots. Carrots are for rabbits and horses, not dragons. While other generations have sold out to China, our generation must see that the Chimerica dream is actually a nightmare—and we are living it.

This China fiction is spread by our supposed business elites, who imagine untold riches if only we love China a little more. They tell us that China is good for business, but their multinational business successes come at the expense of American workers. The United States Chamber of Commerce seems to fight for everything other than the United States and her commerce. They even criticized President Trump for working to redomesticate critical medical manufacturing in the wake of the COVID pandemic. I was surprised to learn that over 90 percent of ibuprofen is made outside our country. Can we not even have an America First headache anymore?

The Chinese story has been a fairy tale, but like a lot of fairy tales it has come to a deadly end—the coronavirus outbreak there leaving an estimated hundred thousand dead in the first few months of 2020 alone, drowning in their own fluids, alone in a hospital bed. Why is it that so many pandemics seem to come from China? Why can't they get it together? Why can't China function like other modern countries? It is not unreasonable to ask these questions.

Motivated by naivete and political correctness, we've looked the other way and played pretend. It's hard to grasp the enormity of the problem. We are outnumbered by the Chinese, and we have lost our focus. Han Chinese is the default setting for the human species—1.3 billion and counting. When you're one in a million in

China, there are still 1,300 just like you. While we've wasted our time and treasure putzing around the Middle East, the Middle Kingdom has grown larger, smarter, and more ambitious. For most of my life, America has chased desert democracy mirages while the Chinese have steadily built positional advantage over their neighbors and us. We've been drained, clumsily attempting to build democracies out of sand, blood, and Arab militias.

Meanwhile, the Chinese have built skyscrapers, aircraft carriers, and supply chains to enhance their might. While we were fretting about the Foreign Corrupt Practices Act, which bans Americans from paying business bribes to Third World countries, the Chinese were showing up with suitcases of cash and ready prostitutes. In the Dominican Republic and the Bahamas—right in our backyard—the Chinese are closing deals. They have been as cunning as we have been clueless. Chinese intelligence professionals know the motives for creating double agents summed up among English speakers by the acronym MICE—money, ideology, coercion, and ego—and they have many promising targets among the global elite. They have found it is easy to corrupt the very people who have been serving as the China-dismissing, clueless storytellers.

When I was a boy, I was taught to feel sorry for the Chinese. My mother would tell me to clean my plate because there were starving kids in China. Their one-child policy meant they sent their daughters—and they were all daughters; Chinese culture is rough on women—abroad for eager American couples to adopt. That is, those who weren't aborted. China was a tragic case and certainly not a great power. We had to be magnanimous to help our Chinese friends up out of poverty. At the end of the twentieth century, there was a Chinese economic miracle, but we lost sight of the cost to the American dream.

Things have changed—fast.

The enormity of the Chinese problem is a modern one, brought on in the last fifty years. Only Nixon could go to China, but it was Henry Kissinger, after traveling there in 1971, who went to work for China and cashed the checks. You're never too old—Kissinger is ninety-seven as I write this—to sell out. There's a lot of green to be had in Red China but none of it is going to go to you. No, you get the bill for the elite's virtue signaling and adventurism.

The former national security advisor and secretary of state even wrote a book titled *On China*, but it really ought to have been titled *Bought by China*. Kissinger would be the first but by no means the last one to have his palm stuffed with China's money. The Chinese pay cash and buy your soul.

What's been good for China has also been good for Kissinger. The architects of America's Chinese policy have had their policies "Made in China" too.

Kissinger headed up China Ventures, a company that partnered with China's state bank but only in projects that "enjoy the unquestioned support of the People's Republic of China." Kissinger has received millions from China and from American businesses hoping to move to China since 1988. *Wall Street Journal* reporter John Fialka wrote an article called "Mr. Kissinger Has Opinions on China—and Business Ties" that detailed some of the cozy relationships Kissinger has enjoyed.

Kissinger even supported the Chinese crackdown in Tiananmen Square and argued against economic sanctions, which would have hurt his bottom line: "China remains too important for America's national security to risk the relationship on the emotions of the moment…. No government in the world would have tolerated having the main square of its capital occupied for eight weeks by tens of thousands of demonstrators," argued Kissinger in a *Washington Post* op-ed in August 1989, just two months after the Chinese government massacred protestors in Tiananmen Square.

Should we really be so surprised? Frauds gravitate toward frauds. And there's little punishment for sellouts. Kissinger's conflicts of interest did not preclude him from having an honored spot among our foreign policy elite.

"The relationship between China and the United States has become a central element in the quest for world peace and global well-being," he wrote in *On China*. To build world peace, he got a piece of every deal.

But has the deal been good for us? And whose peace is it? Globalization is too often sinification, making non-Chinese things more Chinese. We've seen that with the growing number of multinational organizations and companies that depend upon being in China's good graces, from the NBA to NBC. The status quo is China gets richer and we get poorer. This is by design. We let them launder their polluted profits through our real estate markets—and push Americans further and further out into the countryside, where nature is paved and commutes lengthened. Our cities become Chinese playgrounds, our universities their training grounds.

We let the Chinese take seats in institutions meant for Americans, ones supported with tax dollars, because the Chinese pay top dollar to get in. Sometimes they pay more than a little extra. College counselor Rick Singer accepted bribes to get undeserving kids into colleges across the country, but his best customers were Chinese party bosses. One family paid $1.2 million to get their daughter into Yale. Another paid $6.5 million to get their daughter into Stanford. Xi Jinping sent his daughter to Harvard, though how he can afford the $70,000 tuition on an official salary of $13,000 I leave to you to figure out. The FBI accuses our top schools of accepting hundreds of millions in fishy donations—and yet tuition keeps going up year after year for Americans.

President Trump recognized the risk of Chinese infiltration of higher education when he announced from the Rose Garden that student visas from China would be vetted more rigorously. I wonder if they should be here at all. Our professoriat has also been bought off, and some of them have found themselves the witting or unwitting tools of Chinese espionage, a topic we will examine in further detail in the chapter "Big Tech Hates America."

The bipartisan consensus on China has been created by bipartisan payoffs. Whereas the Russians cause chaos, the Chinese open their checkbooks—and find out how cheaply our retired senators can be rented or bought.

In addition to Kissinger, there's former Sen. David Vitter, Republican of Louisiana, who survived a prostitution scandal but lost a gubernatorial campaign, then managed to prostitute himself as a lobbyist for China-based Hikvision. Vitter was secretly recorded promising to do all he could to stop Hikvision from being barred by the Commerce Department. Sen. Vitter co-sponsored a resolution in 2015 that made trade deals contingent on a country's religious freedom record. But lobbyist Vitter has seemingly no problem selling the technology used in China's concentration camps to surveil its Muslim minority. The word "Orwellian" gets thrown around often these days, but helping the Chinese state drum up money from American taxpayers to spy on American citizens is pretty jarring. It turns out David Vitter is far more dangerous as the trick than as the John.

Not to be outdone is former Sen. Max Baucus, Democrat of Montana, who is actually on the board of advisors of Alibaba, a Chinese company that traffics in counterfeit goods. Last year Alibaba settled a $250 million lawsuit for failing to disclose its counterfeit problem to investors. That wasn't all it failed to disclose. Alibaba's CEO Jack Ma promised for years that he wasn't a Communist Party official. Turns out he was a Communist

Party official. Most recently, Baucus got in a spot of trouble for comparing Trump to Hitler on Chinese state TV. One wonders how he justified working for Chinese companies that make the equipment necessary for real modern-day concentration camps. Vice President Biden personally advocated for Baucus to serve as U.S. ambassador to China during the Obama/Biden administration. One wonders what position Biden would offer Baucus if he had the chance again.

Joe Biden is the classic China First American politician. The Biden Center at the University of Pennsylvania may have China connections that would make even the Clinton Foundation blush!

According to a much-cited National Legal and Policy Center (NLPC) complaint, UPenn has systemically failed to report China gifts and contracts, despite a pesky provision of the Higher Education Act that requires disclosure of foreign gifts exceeding $250,000. Converting Chinese money into Chinese influence on American policy is big business for some of our nation's most ivy-draped universities. For Biden, this was perfect. He set up the Biden Center as "a place where policymakers here and abroad will know they can be in touch with some of the best minds."

As is typical with Biden, more may be getting touched than we originally knew. The Washington Free Beacon's Alana Goodman connects the dots:

> The Biden Cancer Initiative, which had $2.1 million in total assets in 2018 before suspending its operations [in 2019], according to its tax records, declined to provide a list of donors. The Biden Institute at the University of Delaware has also declined to reveal its funders.
>
> While the Penn Biden Center has not released information on its donors, foreign funding to the University of Pennsylvania has risen more than threefold since its soft

opening, spiking to over $100 million last year from $31 million in 2016, according to Department of Education records. China has been the largest contributor during that time...

The donations included a $502,750 "monetary gift" in October 2017 from the State Administration of Foreign Experts Affairs, a Chinese government agency that helps administer the regime's "Thousand Talents Plan." Federal prosecutors claim the program is linked to Chinese espionage operations at American universities and have prosecuted academics for hiding their involvement in it...

Penn received a total of 23 anonymous gifts from China between March 2017 and the end of 2019, totaling over $21 million. In the preceding four years, the university had disclosed just five anonymous donations from China, totaling less than $5 million.

There may be a perfectly good explanation for why the Biden Center's affiliation with UPenn coincided with a tripling of Chinese cash to the school, much of it delivered anonymously. But there is no excuse for UPenn violating black letter transparency laws intended to protect us all. I've joined NLPC in calling for a review of these shady transactions. If in fact the Biden Center is yet another in a string of international money-laundering operations to facilitate political power, this could be the most damaging Biden scandal yet. It is just all too common.

Sen. Joe Lieberman, a former Democratic vice presidential candidate, once shared the slogan "Leadership for the New Millennium. Prosperity for America's Families" with Al Gore. Today, Lieberman works for China's ZTE, a company that routinely flouts U.S. sanctions on Iran and North Korea and paid a $1 billion fine. Sen. Lieberman called the 5G operator a national security threat, but lobbyist Lieberman is happy to work the phones and give them a "security" review—whatever that means.

If lobbyist Lieberman ever completes that "security" review, he should conclude that our national security comes from understanding that ours is a nation that values its rights and fights to maintain them. China doesn't share our concerns about human rights, animal rights, copyrights, or really any kind of rights because they don't understand the notion of rights. If the government can kick you out of your property without just compensation, you don't own it. The absence of ownership isn't progressive but regressive and brings about even more of the income inequality supposedly derided by the political Left.

So why is China favored by American liberals? *New York Times* columnist Tom Friedman wished America could be China for a day. "China's one-party autocracy can impose the important policies needed to move a society forward in the twenty-first century," Friedman wrote admiringly in 2009. Billionaire and Google investor Mike Moritz celebrated the slavish society he saw before him in a piece titled, "Silicon Valley Would Be Wise to Follow China's Lead."

> *In China…it is quite usual for the management of 10 and 15-year-old companies to have working dinners followed by two or three meetings. If u Chinese company schedules tasks for the weekend, nobody complains about missing a Little League game or skipping a basketball outing with friends. Little wonder it is a common sight at a Chinese company to see many people with their heads resting on their desks taking a nap in the early afternoon.*

Our elites have seen the future and it works—for them. Chinese workers are as the American elite hoped we Americans might become: compliant, voiceless, interchangeable, and therefore expendable. Faced with the coronavirus outbreak, the American Left was only too happy to import the lockdowns that Communist China forced on its people indefinitely. But Americans resisted and disobeyed because we believe in liberty or death. There are things worth dying for, after all.

To the elites we are all interchangeable—just labor, a commodity even. We don't have any specialness or any habits of free people that make us separate and unique. This idea of the substitutable nature of people means we can invade Afghanistan, Iraq, or Syria and turn them into Jeffersonian Democrats. All you need are some institutions and some platitudes about human rights and free markets will work out.

But such a view undervalues what makes America great: her people and her habits. Our foreign policy elites don't take seriously how different we are from the rest of the world and how precious the institutions that we've built up over centuries are.

WE ARE NOT AND NEVER WILL BE CHINESE; THEY ARE NOT AND never will be a free people.

The Chinese Communist Party has always been despotic. This is what the neoconservatives get wrong. The neocons separate the world into panda-cuddlers (the liberals) and dragon-slayers (them). I am neither a hawk nor a dove but an eagle, and I can see clearly and at a distance what we have to do. We should do all we can to help China's neighbors avoid being turned into Chinese serfs economically. It is they we should trade with (on fair terms for our people). Thailand, Taiwan, Singapore, South Korea, Indonesia, and Vietnam all seek to avoid Chinese dominion. The enemy of my enemy can be my friend. Containment breeds alliances. Nations that share our priorities and our values are our friends; nations that share neither are our foes. The world's largest consumer market, which is still the U.S., will find plenty of people willing to meet its needs. We don't need China; China needs us. That's why they buy our politicians.

China has had tremendous economic growth and yet their air is toxic, and their rivers polluted. They dump their trash into the world's oceans and don't give a damn. We should tax their goods and brand it the Chinese carbon tax. You should not be able to poison the air in Shanghai so you can buy a penthouse in Manhattan.

Our political class has been so wrong about China because they were too busy getting rich to get smart. Only when we stop the former can we do the latter. How wrong have they been? Look at a few examples.

The internet will not make China free. Tim Wu's book, *The Master Switch*, teaches us that while technology may start out naively libertarian, it always ends up centralizing power. All technology means is doing more with less. Technology doesn't necessarily mean freedom. You can have more totalitarianism with less effort. That too is a sort of technological advance. It wasn't supposed to be this way, they told us. The internet would inevitably make China move toward democracy. "Good luck," President Clinton joked about Chinese efforts to censor the internet in March 2000. "That's sort of like trying to nail Jell-O to the wall."

But the country that built the Great Wall had no problem nailing the proverbial Jell-O to it. Indeed, Chinese control of the internet bled into American companies as well, with YouTube censoring videos critical of the Chinese state. Google has even proposed working with the Chinese military instead of working with ours. "In China, there is pretty much only one rule, and it is simple: Don't undermine the state. So titans like Weibo and Baidu heed censorship orders," writes Raymond Zhong of the *New York Times*. "Unwanted beliefs and ideologies are kept out."

Share the wrong meme or tweet the wrong thing and you and your family can be shut out of polite society through China's social credit system, which bears an uncanny resemblance to Big Tech's effort to shadowban and suspend American conservatives. The East German Stasi dreamed of such power, but in China, it is extremely routine. China's walled-in tech world gives them serious advantages. When you have a billion people, you collect a lot of data. That data can be mined and trained through artificial intelligence. The insights gleaned can be weaponized without a human even passing judgment. You can build authoritarianism through algorithms.

Naturally, China seeks to expand its reach globally through its technology. Globalization is sinification, after all.

The Commerce Department has barred some forty or so companies from doing business here, including most famously Huawei. They need to ban a lot more, including TikTok and drone manufacturer DJI. Throw in BGI, who massively discount their genetic sequencing technology to build up a database of genomes for experimentation and analysis. Just as the China virus COVID-19 turns our immune system against our bodies, so too does the broader Chinese attack on America alter what is supposed to be good into evil.

We should restrict federal contracting to companies that have an anti-Chinese espionage policy and undergo background checks by the FBI. The Chinese cannot be allowed to use LinkedIn to spy on American companies as recently detailed by the *New York Times*. Amazon, Microsoft, and Google are among a number of American companies that are still providing web services to black-listed Chinese surveillance firms. That includes Zoom, which hosts its servers in China.

Fortunately, China has laid out their playbook for us. They are making state-directed investments in key areas in a way we would be wise to copy: artificial intelligence, genomics, and drone technology. We should take the Chinese seriously and take seriously what they say their aims are. We can frustrate their objectives precisely because they telegraph their punches and issue state directives. What they cannot learn they steal. What they cannot steal they bribe or buy. We must block these sales and undo the bad sales already done, particularly in the areas where the Chinese have expressed great interest. The Obama regime should never have allowed BGI to buy Complete Genomics, and we should not allow DJI or TikTok to compete in the United States.

We must keep secret our advances and even entertain classified patents. This'll mean sourcing more technologies away from the universities and Big Tech, instead trusting and empowering American companies and engineers. We beat the Soviet Union by out-innovating them and by making sure we always kept the informational advantage. We can make so many impressive things that the Chinese can't possibly steal it all, but we must see to it that the greatest minds of our generation are not wasted merely clicking ads or liking photos. Our best minds should be working on bold ideas for the national betterment—just as China's already are.

It doesn't matter whether you believe the Wuhan virus started in a lab or in the wet markets. China behaved negligently. Where China misbehaves, we should send our trial lawyers after them and map out what they own here. The Chinese elite—and they are all in the government over there—send their kids here and own property. That gives us leverage, though. We must never allow our children to be placed under house arrest by the Wuhan virus and made into de facto Uighurs, begging a high-tech central authority to be let out of their homes.

Free men and women breathe air that is both free and nontoxic, while their kids fish in clean rivers as they please. But to remain free, we must think clearly about the problems we face before it is too late. The price of freedom—and enduring American exceptionalism—is vigilance, not wishful storytelling.

CHAPTER TEN

SPORTS FAN

I LOVE SPORTS. MY OWN BASEBALL CAREER ENDED EARLY DUE TO a lack of talent. Now in my late thirties, watching sports isn't some nostalgic look back at "the glory days." For me there were few to none. Sports allow those of us who grew up too fat, too slow, or too uncoordinated to admire talent in others that we do not ourselves possess.

Unjealous admiration of our fellow Americans who can do things we can only dream of is heartwarming and unifying. We end up loving them even though we don't know them (we do the same with politicians, but I digress). Jerseys of all-stars are purchased; posters appear on our children's bedroom walls. We internalize our affiliation with the achievements of our favorite teams and players. "I believe that *we* will win!" We are part of the team. Don't wash the lucky jersey! Our cheers and jeers through the television matter, we tell ourselves. The coaching advice we hurl from bleachers is impactful. It must be heard and precisely followed.

Perhaps there is a reason sports and politics so often collide. Both have become more tribal than our religion or the competing companies where we work. After all, aren't we all more likely to switch jobs and work for our competitor than we are to ever become a *Yankees* fan? Are we surprised, then, that race and sports and politics often end up as featured ingredients in the gumbo of our spiciest national conversations?

Sports are a force for good in America. In 2006, I spent a semester taking classes at Florida State University Law School to accommodate jobs in the Florida Legislature and at the Republican Party of Florida. My boss was then state House speaker and sports superfan Marco Rubio. And, yes, we all knew Marco was a special political talent then, though we did have trouble finding him during one intense budget negotiation while the Miami Dolphins were on the draft clock.

One of my best friends this semester was FSU basketball's starting wing, Jason Rich. Seeing sports through his eyes gave me perspective on life I appreciate to this day. Basketball got Jason paid and laid. He was the best player on an ACC team—what would you expect? Mostly, though, it got him out and up. Sports was his opportunity and my friend seized it.

Jason and I had been asked to join a diverse group of student leaders at FSU. We met every Monday night at the law firm of now-famed civil rights attorney Ben Crump, one of the group's founders during his student tenure. Ben was always generous to mentor and encourage his fellow Seminoles. Ben Crump would become the third financial contributor to my campaign for state representative in 2010. "We don't agree on much, Matt. But we love FSU—and I'm counting on you to be a leader for all people, not just those who agree with you," he said as he wrote out two thousand dollars in donations.

You always remember those who were with you at the beginning. As I write, Ben and his partner Daryl Parks continue to productively discuss proposals to improve policing with me. I'm glad they do. It makes me better to listen, even when I don't agree.

Jason Rich and I studied leadership together, prayed together, ate and drank together, smoked together, and chased women together. He lent me his couch when I struck out at the night-clubs (not a rare occurrence). I memorized the names of his eight siblings over a weekend with friends at my family home in Seaside, Florida. Through all the fun, I've never observed a more driven human. Excellence in athletics comes from intense personal sacrifice. Perhaps we mythologize athletes so much because they can do so much that the rest of us can't.

Jason and I grew up fifty miles and a world apart. I was in lily-white Niceville, Jason in a mostly nonwhite area on the outskirts of Pensacola; both are in my current congressional district. Jason always knew he was going to excel in basketball— that was the easy part for him. Like fellow Pensacola Seminole guard Ralph Mims, he was ultimately plucked out of North-west Florida and enrolled in a prestigious prep school for future professional athletes.

Harder for my buddy was thinking about life for his siblings— how, without sports, he'd be hustling on the street. It was a sort of survivor's guilt that drove Jason to lead in other aspects of his life. While he had a few too many knee surgeries to make it in the NBA beyond off-season scrimmages, Jason made money deploying his craft in Europe and across the world. He still calls from Rome, Athens, and Switzerland to discuss investment ideas—always with the goal of benefiting his family in Pensacola.

Many professional athletes, like Jason, are black. They have a perspective on black life in America that many they interact with don't—including me. They shouldn't get siloed as "athletes" that have somehow surrendered their right to social and political activism.

More people should be engaged in our politics, not less. I don't have a right to tell athletes to stay out of politics any more than they have a right to shut down obsessive sports fan internet message boards. They have a far greater right to be in "my lane" than I do theirs. That doesn't mean I have to agree with their political views any more than they indulge my perspective on the absurdity of the sacrifice bunt. Why give up a precious out?!

Kneeling during the national anthem is an overgeneralized indictment of America. I won't support any athlete or sports league that participates. The un-woke version of Drew Brees was right—it is "disrespectful" to those who have loved this country enough to die for her. America is the greatest nation that has ever existed. Just ask everyone trying to break in. Sure, we've made horrible mistakes. All nations do. Our founders recognized we would always strive to be a more perfect union, and we still must. I'm talking about improving policing, specifically.

Refusing to stand for a great nation is not a sign of strength, but of naivete over the blessing that comes with being born an American of any race, background, sexual orientation, gender, or creed. Americans are the peers of kings—we should treat ourselves and one another with respect.

Sans overgeneralizing that America is a horrid, racist nation, protesting over policing concerns doesn't bother me, sports or no sports.

Following Michael Brown's death in Ferguson, Missouri, St. Louis Rams players were motivated to be heard. As they were announced before kickoff one game, some came out of the tunnel with their hands raised in the "Hands up, don't shoot!" gesture. Athletes should be able to use their platform like this. They were making a real point about an event and a tragic outcome.

By contrast, riots following the murder of George Floyd in June 2020 were not a form of protected political speech. It isn't "protest" when you're throwing a cinder block through the window of a Nike store and walking out with a pair of Air Jordans. Politics doesn't demand that any of us rob a Cheesecake Factory or burn houses of worship. This wasn't the politics of reformers; it was the thuggery of a permanent criminal element. It wasn't appreciated by George Floyd's brother, either.

I believe God worked through Philonise Floyd. I told him that during a hearing of the House Judiciary Committee. He had rejected calls to defund the police, condemned destructive riots, and shared deep, sincere empathy with the victims, citing the words of Martin Luther King. We had a productive discussion about policing reform during the formal and informal hearing moments. Perhaps it helped that his attorney was none other than Ben Crump.

I'm listening, Ben.

THE LATE JOSÉ FERNÁNDEZ WILL ALWAYS BE MY FAVORITE MAJOR league pitcher. A fire fastball with movement. A slider that left hitters with gumby knees. A changeup that dove down and in on righties and fell off the table for lefties. He could hit, too. The Marlins, without payroll for a competitive starting lineup much less quality reserves, would even use him to pinch-hit—almost unheard of for an ace pitcher. Tragically, he died in a boating accident that killed three people, possibly a result of his cocaine use. I'll remember him for how he lived.

Fernández was jailed as a teenager for trying to escape Communist Cuba. He finally got out, went to high school in Florida, and got drafted by the Marlins, my favorite team. The vitality and joy he brought to baseball cannot be adequately addressed in this book. He was electric in every way. His pitching performances sold out stadiums even when the team around him was otherwise hard to watch.

I fell in love with Jose Fernández when I saw a documentary chronicling his U.S. citizenship ceremony. He said that being
an all-star MLB pitcher wasn't his proudest achievement—being
an American was. I often saw the experience of José Fernández
through the lens of my own son.

Well, I say son. It's complicated.

Nestor arrived in Tallahassee from Cuba when he was twelve.
He didn't speak a word of English. He had waited eight years to
come to America legally. Finally, the approval for him and his
mother had been granted, but she didn't make the flight. She would
die ten days later in Cuba. Her trip to the consulate to pick up the
visas would be her last heroic foray from her deathbed following a
long, terminal battle with breast cancer. She had gotten him on the
plane, to a new life in America.

I had been dating Nestor's sister May for six months. We
fell in love quickly. She and I even conspired to smuggle some
life-extending drugs onto the Communist island where people die
who shouldn't. I'd thank the Cuban-born doctor who helped us by
name, but I'm not certain the Board of Medicine has a statute of
limitations for conspiracy to smuggle drugs into Cuba. Most of
the drugs are heading the other direction.

May was the successful events director at a capitol city restaurant. I ended up holding lots of events there. My dear friend and
fellow State Representative Brad Drake told me, "She must be
one of the ten best-looking women in Florida—and this is one
good-looking state."

My Spanish was rusty—it would get better—but sports is an
international language. When I first met Nestor I brought two
gloves and a baseball. He brought an outsized hug. After playing
in the park, he asked May and me, "*Somos una familia?*" We were
family, I assured him with tears welling in my eyes. That was seven
years ago.

May and I didn't work out for reasons more my doing than hers. She has continued her career and we remain close friends. Nestor lives with me and has just graduated high school. Though we share no blood, and no legal paperwork defines our family relationship, he is my son in every sense of the word. I could not imagine loving him more. He will enroll in university to pursue a nursing degree in the fall. His achievements are my own proudest moments on earth.

During a heated debate on police reform in the House Judiciary Committee, Rep. Cedric Richmond essentially argued that white legislators should stop offering amendments and vote "no" if we so chose because this was about people of color—not us. He talked about his experience with his black son as something we could never understand.

I asked how he could be so sure none of us had raised nonwhite children. He replied that if I had a nonwhite son he was fighting for my family harder than I was. Understandably, this set me off. "Who the hell do you think you are?" I loudly exclaimed.

This exchange led to the world knowing about Nestor. Until then, we had chosen to spare him from the hate of politics. Now a nineteen-year-old rising university freshman, he is publicly as much a part of my life as he has been privately for years. Seeing how well he has taken to his newfound notoriety reinforces my belief that he will be ready for whatever life, or even university, might throw his way.

I saw the news that José Fernández died on ESPN from a D.C. hotel room. Nestor and I were texting. I wasn't a congressman yet but soon would be after my noncompetitive general election. Fernández was Nestor's favorite player too. We always watched his games together.

When ESPN switched from the news of Fernández's death to the Kaepernick kneeling protests, I was triggered...and soon tweeting. "To all who will kneel during the anthem today—just remember how Jose Fernandez risked his life for the chance to stand for it." Instant outrage! I was only a candidate for Congress but had already made my first Washington headlines.

"Racist!" proclaimed the woke Left and Twitter blue-check-mark brigade. The PC police had an apprehension in progress. Screw them. I stand by the tweet. Let the first person who calls me a racist sign up to raise a nonwhite immigrant child. The inter-section of sports, politics, and race would be my first "Washington controversy." It would also generate my first prime-time national cable hit.

The Tax Cuts and Jobs Act was being debated in 2017, Trump's first year in office, and around the same time my frustration with the NFL was growing, as Fox's Tucker Carlson would soon notice.

Jerry Jones, the Dallas Cowboys owner, was kneeling at the fifty-yard line during the national anthem, submitting to the cancel culture. The NFL was growing much more comfortable with these overly generalized indictments, ending the days of the NFL representing the most positive, optimistic view of this country. Shahid Khan, owner of the Jaguars, even allowed players to stand for "God Save the Queen" while in London yet kneel for the American Anthem. Did Kahn think that the sun never set on the British empire absent some serious colonization and oppres-sion? America fights for the freedom of others, not always with the Brits throughout history.

Inspired by such outrages—not to mention basic fairness to all taxpayers—I filed an amendment to Trump's bold tax bill saying the NFL should not get special tax breaks. Tucker Carlson took note and booked me for one question in the final thirty seconds of the show. My amendment was not adopted, but my accountant and friend Steve Riggs texted me to say he was confident that my brief appearance would not be my last. Steve is apparently great at all kinds of projections, not just revenue models.

I still think there are great Americans associated with the NFL, such as Miami Dolphins owner Stephen Ross, who donates to both parties—sometimes when he wants things, sometimes just on a whim, but regardless, he had his name on a fundraiser for the Trump campaign, willing to aid the cause even though people started boycotting SoulCycle and other businesses he owns. To his credit, he put out a statement saying he wouldn't back down—and recently the Dolphins also drafted Tua Tagovailoa, the best quarterback in the region since Marino. So maybe I'll give the NFL another chance.

SPORTS INCREASE PEOPLE'S SENSE OF CAMARADERIE. I GOT invited to go see the World Series appearance by the Washington Nationals with the president and his family and others, and I remember my mentor, Rep. Mark Meadows of North Carolina, saying to Trump that he had just heard ISIS leader Abu Bakr al-Baghdadi had been killed. Meadows opined that Trump would now be less likely to be impeached. This struck me and, I think, the president as flattery, masquerading as unfounded optimism. We might love Trump, but it would be silly to pretend the Democrats ever will.

First Lady Melania Trump, in stark contrast, said the Democrats would now have to impeach her husband just to show that they still have the power to do so. I had said much the same thing during an appearance on Hill.TV, and it struck me that in this instance my cynical view of politics had a bit more in common with the First Lady than with Meadows's genial hopes.

Luckily, the president understands that power in politics is not an end unto itself unless you're helping people. His jovial tone, which his supporters sense behind his occasional toughness but his detractors somehow don't, is born of a hope that ultimately Americans are all on the same team, and if he can lead us to victory, in ways big or small, he'll be proud of it. He literally wants us all to win, not just to prove he's the team captain.

Take his handling of the coronavirus crisis. Regardless of how you weigh the risks involved—and few of us can pretend to be certain about all the science behind such estimates, not even the scientists—you should recognize that Trump could have seized the occasion to play dictator if he had wanted to. Instead, most of the criticism he got during the early months of the crisis was for being hands-off, letting different states try different approaches and, as always, listening to some clashing and dissenting voices about how to handle things.

Given how desperate people become for an authoritarian hand during a crisis, he probably could have nationalized businesses—and then insisted that you check in with a host of new bureaucracies in Washington if you want to work, eat, get closer than six feet to your friends or family, or make a doctor's appointment. But on this occasion, as in the Graham-Cassidy bill that Trump helped craft to repeal and replace Obamacare, his instincts were far removed from those of a dictator or strongman. His first impulse is to get Washington out of the way, devolving power to the states and local communities.

The Trump approach to immigration and trade negotiation, which to liberals and libertarians alike might look like exercises of pure power, are better thought of as motivated by something akin to team spirit. If you don't want Washington harassing and controlling your people, even less do you want foreign governments and corporations deciding our destiny.

When I visit the wall the president is resolutely building on our porous southern border, when I see the rampant crime—drugs, beheadings, human trafficking—that increasingly spills across the border, I don't find myself thinking the efforts of the wall-builders and the Border Patrol are aimed at harming another team. Their efforts are aimed, like the president's, at doing right by the home team.

As well-intentioned as police in Mexico or corporate executives in China may seem to some, they're not giving their all to make sure our team comes out on top. They naturally have other priorities. We have our own, and if you call them nationalist, you're not describing something terribly strange, dangerous, or alien. You're describing the same natural impulse that animates and bonds a typical sports team. Maybe that's why, to the horror of America's liberal intellectuals and journalists, nationalism and patriotism come as naturally as watching the Super Bowl to vast swaths of Middle America.

The nineteenth-century Scottish anthropologist John Ferguson McLennan argued that even as societies progress from more primitive to more complex forms, they retain rituals that have "totemic" power because they connote the very formation of the society itself: its people. The people cannot and should not try to replicate the exact conditions of their founding. No going back to living in caves or, in the case of the United States, in cabins without floors or running water. But it is natural to revel in the ceremonies, the victories, the informal quasi-religion that reminds us we are still one people.

Newcomers are not always to be shunned, but they will have to prove themselves, like new teammates on a top-tier sports team. Don't tell me that's hard to understand, that it doesn't jibe with some of your most basic intuitions. Don't tell me that it's hateful. It's respect for that which has been built over long years by tacit partnership among a very large and dynamic team of collaborators. It is normal to want that team of some 330 million to thrive and perfectly normal to be peeved at those who insult it, tear it down, or don't really want to be a working part of it at all.

No team is perfectly homogeneous. It shouldn't be. But we should not be so reductive as to equate team "diversity" with race or gender alone. Humans are diverse based on how they grew up, where they live, how they solve problems, how they learn, and how they process information, among many other things. A functioning team has to be flexible, has to make use of the differing capabilities and perspectives of its members. There is room for dissent even on a loving and cooperative team. But if you're there to sabotage it, and there are times when some activists give that impression, I will be there to call you out.

I was fighting for a team called America when I made that first Tucker Carlson appearance. If you saw it and heard a hint of anger, I'm sure you also sensed the love. If you're a sports fan, you're familiar with that combination.

CHAPTER ELEVEN

A BIRTHRIGHT WORTH DEFENDING

"Restricted immigration is not an offensive but purely a defensive action. It is not adopted in criticism of others in the slightest degree but solely for the purpose of protecting ourselves. We cast no aspersions on any race or creed, but we must remember that every object of our institutions of society and government will fail unless America be kept American."

—Calvin Coolidge, accepting the Republican
presidential nomination, August 14, 1924

I'M OFTEN ASKED HOW I JUGGLE THE RESPONSIBILITIES OF FUNC-tionally being a Fox News volunteer contributor with that of a congressman. It's easy to go on Fox. It's work to go on CNN, but it's pure joy to go on MSNBC. Where else is every question about how racist you are? Predictable TV is boring TV. And I don't do boring.

And so it was with MSNBC host Chris Hayes who, on January 16, 2018, tried to pigeonhole me as—wait for it—a racist for thinking that America should have an immigration policy that puts American needs ahead of foreign ones. Immigration, unique among political issues, reveals just how out of touch the radical Left really is. Of course, it's hard to be in touch when you never touch the public. The Left's coalition is increasingly high tech, high finance, and higher education—institutions highly unlikely to be displaced by illegal immigrant labor.

The way it works on MSNBC is that the host has to simultaneously virtue signal to his viewing base while trying to cause drama between you and the president. They stopped reporting the news long ago and seek instead to make news through opinion. Hayes or Maddow—to be honest, it's hard to tell them apart—will furrow his/her brow and shake his/her head and ask you why it was that the president was so hurtful, so offensive, so beyond the pale, so [insert focus-group-tested word du jour].

The standard Republican shtick is to agree with the president without necessarily agreeing with his language or his tone. You know the drill. We agree without endorsing. The host sputters and putters and then breaks for commercial. Lots of heat, not lots of light. The moment is over so fast that it's sometimes as if it never happened. I try to make every unforgiving minute count.

I gave the standard reply, at least at first. I was new and still learning.

"I would not pick those terms, but I would say that the conditions in Haiti are deplorable, they are disgusting," I said. "I mean, everywhere you look in Haiti, it's sheet metal and garbage when I was there."

Hayes hit back, stuttering from my candor. He wasn't used to it. "I would suggest that people would find that kind of characterization, where people live, have pride, and love the place they're from, as derogatory."

"Look, there are very bad conditions in Haiti. It's accurate," I replied with a smile. "Go there. Look around."

Look around. Draw your own conclusions. Use your own mind. After all, as President Trump said, we don't have time for political correctness. The first duty of being an intellectual elite is to tell the truth, but it isn't that hard when you can easily see the truth for yourself. We've all seen the videos of illegal aliens streaming across our borders. We're not streaming across theirs. There is a reason. It is better here, and everyone but our elites knows it.

The president called me afterward. He enjoys the show, especially when his best rhetorical gladiators go beyond the friendly confines of Fox News and battle the far edges of the Left.

"You're a wise guy, Gaetz. You'll always be a wise guy. But you are very sharp. Quick. You are a wise guy and a wise man."

But you don't have to be particularly wise to use your eyes. No, we don't really do the whole moral and cultural relativism thing, the president and I. America is simply the best country. That's why so many people try to break in.

The Haitians agree and have voted with their feet. There are at least a million Haitians living in America, some legally, some not, most in my beloved state of Florida. The Clinton Foundation robbed them of the full potential of hurricane relief funds so that the State Department's "Friend of Bill" contacts would be awarded lucrative contracts. The Obama regime gave "temporary"—ha!—protected status to some two hundred thousand Haitians illegally in the U.S. in 2010.

You don't typically do that when things are going swimmingly in the old country. After all, following Chris Hayes's horrified gasping during our interview, Haiti descended into violence exacerbated by a corrupt president and horrendous living conditions for its people. Now it's sheet metal and garbage…and blood.

President Barack Obama took the liberty to quote James Madison, saying, "[T]he most important office in a democracy" is "citizen." But he did everything in his power to cheapen the meaning of American citizenship. Perhaps that's because he considered himself a "citizen of the world," as he put it to a crowd of two hundred thousand adoring fans in Berlin. Schoolchildren may pledge their allegiance to the republic, but the last president didn't see fit to offer them reciprocal allegiance by protecting their future from the consequences of unchecked illegal immigration. Loyalty is a two-way street.

When I pledge allegiance, I mean it. To my friends, to my family, but most of all, to my country. America First means American Citizens First, not the roaring crowds of European nations growing weaker due to their own flawed immigration choices and cultural decadence. If Europe is a glimpse at the Woketopia, count me out.

American citizenship makes us the "peers of kings," as Coolidge once said, so why is seemingly everyone trying to give away our birthright? Or dilute the preciousness of Americanism? Many politicians frame the immigration issue in terms of its financial cost or impact on economic growth. But immigration policy in America really isn't about money. To us, it's about our cherished American identity. To them, it's about power.

The real reason Democrats support unlimited illegal immigration is that they see unlimited potential to use illegal immigrants to hold onto power indefinitely. The immigrants first become clients of the administrative state, climbing aboard (and thus straining) social safety nets designed by Americans, paid for by Americans, and meant to help Americans.

Left-wing "grassroots" groups and liberal politicians prioritize connecting illegal immigrants with taxpayer-funded programs, which the Democrats run, ultimately converting the programs' users into Democrat voters. In two-party democracies, there is always one party that seeks to expand the franchise so as to expand its power. Eventually, the expansion leads to democratic collapse, followed by tyranny. Such efforts necessarily dilute the meaning of citizenship and turn us all into subjects of a failing government.

Today's elites would rather import a new people than serve the people that they've already got—people they have too often failed. Barack Obama wasn't the first politician to betray the citizenry, nor will he be the last. In the pre-Civil War period, the South imported slaves partly to keep the Congress proslavery. The more slaves you brought in, the more the slave states would keep their power. The North, recognizing this electoral reality, agreed to the Three-Fifths Compromise by which slaves were counted as three-fifths of a free person for voting purposes rather than as full citizens as in the North. The Three-Fifths Clause, long derided by the Left as demeaning to black people, was actually an anti-slavery compromise that limited the power of the slaveholders.

The Southern states wanted to count slaves as free men but not let them live as free men. They were simultaneously political participants and property. The tension between slavery and freedom in a republic whose founding charter states that all are created equal could not be maintained, and a very bloody civil war became the only way out. After that war, Congress passed the Fourteenth Amendment to make clear that the sons of the Confederacy and former slaves were equal under the law and "subject to the jurisdiction" of the United States when they were born.

Now, I'm just a country lawyer, but then again, so was Andrew Jackson, Abraham Lincoln, and Calvin Coolidge, so I had to turn to the original text to see for myself. The best thing about Congress is that you can look to the congressional record and parse what they were thinking at the time. As often is the case, someone else had already done the legwork. The cool thing about being a lawyer is that you get points for unoriginality, which is kind of what originalism really is. Did you do the history reading? No? Better find a nerd who has. And when it comes to birthright citizenship, there are no better nerds than those of the Claremont Institute.

The Claremont fellow and former Trump national security official Michael Anton has beaten me to the birthright citizenship research. Anton notes the role played by Sen. Jacob Howard of Michigan, who worked with Lincoln to pass the Thirteen Amendment, which outlawed slavery, and the Fourteenth Amendment, which made the newly freed blacks citizens:

> [E]very person born within the limits of the United States, and subject to their jurisdiction, is by virtue of natural law and national law a citizen of the United States. This will not, of course, include persons born in the United States who are foreigners, aliens, who belong to the families of ambassadors or foreign ministers accredited to the government of the United States, but will include every other class of person.

So particular was the Fourteenth Amendment that it specifically excluded Native Americans. Why? Because they weren't under our jurisdiction. (That would have to wait until after Calvin Coolidge passed the Indian Naturalization Act of 1924 and extended citizenship to Native Americans still living on reservations.)

This jurisdictional question is rather obvious when you think about it. British Prime Minister Boris Johnson, born in the United States, can't be prime minister and still run for president. It's nice to think that my father's political hero, Winston Churchill, born to an American mum, could've been president, but he was quintessentially British. Texas transplants like Sen. Ted Cruz (born in Canada) and Congressman Dan Crenshaw (born in Scotland) to American parents are subject to the jurisdiction of America, and so they too can run for president. I suspect both will.

No, the Fourteenth Amendment was about making slaves free. There are only two ways to become American—"by natural law or by national law," by blood or by choice. We trivialize both paths by allowing our courts and think tanks to undermine those legal categories in the service of the corporate slave power. For while the Civil War ended legal slavery, illegal slavery—human trafficking—continues to be rampant, if not wholly unabated. Once again, business and political interests want to count virtual slaves as free people for the purposes of keeping power.

Under a misreading of the Constitution by our Supreme Court, the Department of Commerce counts illegal aliens for the purposes of congressional apportionment. Bring in as many illegal aliens as you want, the federal government implicitly says to the states. The more you bring in, the more you get to keep and expand your power in the House of Representatives. Sound familiar?

There are boroughs throughout the U.S. where there are few voters but tons of illegal aliens. To have a say, all those aliens need to do is have a kid who—under a mistaken understanding of the Constitution—becomes a citizen. It's big business birthing babies in America. Victoria Kim and Frank Shyong reported in the *Los Angeles Times* on a raid against one such practice where "for fees starting at $38,000, the ['maternity tourism' hospital] guides pregnant women through the process." The details have to be quoted to be believed.

"[The] U.S. might refuse entry [if] the belly is too big," one business stated on its website, advising women to travel at twenty-four to thirty weeks into their pregnancy, according to an affidavit. "The size of the belly is quite important to determine when you should arrive in Los Angeles."

The businesses, known as "maternity hotels" or "birthing centers," present a headache for local government and law enforcement because it is not necessarily illegal for foreign nationals to give birth in the U.S. Many agencies openly advertise services offering assistance in getting newborns a U.S. passport and extolling the benefits that come with American citizenship, including public education and immigration benefits for parents.

Chinese scammers, finally charged under the Trump administration, weren't subtle. They called one corrupt organization of this kind You Win USA. According to indictments charging such criminal enterprises, three businesses sold the benefits of giving birth in America, which has "the most attractive nationality," "better air" than China, "priority for jobs in U.S. government" (just what you want from a country with a history of spying on us), superior educational resources that include "free education from junior high school to public high school," a more stable political situation, and the potential to "receive your senior supplement benefits when you are living overseas."

AMERICA IS NOT JUST A CONSTITUTION, IDEA, OR SET OF VALUES. America is our home. And we must do everything to protect our home.

During a trip to the U.S.-Mexico border in Yuma, Arizona, I met patriotic Americans working in the U.S. Border Patrol. If she had her way, my colleague AOC would fire them all and denigrate the role they play in safeguarding our home from uninvited intruders. Almost all were of Hispanic heritage. They spoke with disgust of cartel leaders who would sneak their baby mamas (or is it baby *mamacitas*?) across the border late in pregnancy so that their children—proven to be the next generation of cartel talent—would have the trappings and legal benefits of American citizenship. El Chapo's sons and fellow cartel bosses' sons are Americans by law. The greatest nation in human history is getting played—and rather easily—by Third World narcos.

Indeed, every single one of the children born in these criminals' care is as American as you or me. Or so the defenders of birthright citizenship—really a form of fraud—would have you believe. Nobody knows how many children become citizens in this way, but the State Department estimates that "thousands of children" are born in the U.S. each year to people who are either visiting or conducting business on nonimmigrant visas. This isn't "One man, one vote" but Boss Tweed-style politics where criminal organizations take advantage of what our ruling elite's asinine abstractions permit. Don't hate the players. Hate the game. Then change it.

But there are few who want to change the game. They play word games instead. The language of immigration itself is designed to obfuscate reality. An "undocumented" immigrant may, the language implies, become documented. They didn't break in without permission—they're just missing some paperwork. A "migrant" sounds like someone who can't be stopped by a border any more than you can stop the migration of birds or the butterflies. Pulitzer Prize-winning journalist—and illegal immigrant—Jose Antonio Vargas even wrote a book whose subtitle, *Notes of an Undocumented Citizen*, highlighted the oxymoron.

The Left often talks about the "stakeholders" in a community whenever there's a project they don't like, but they seem positively incurious about how unchecked immigration affects the body politic. The research has been extensive. Professor George Borjas of Harvard—we won't hold that affiliation against him—who is himself an immigrant, has shown that increased legal and illegal immigration has consequences. "Wage trends over the past half-century suggest that a 10 percent increase in the number of workers with a particular set of skills probably lowers the wage of that group by at least 3 percent," he wrote for Politico.

Borjas estimates that the wealth transfer from American employees displaced by illegal immigration to their American employers is enormous, roughly half a trillion a year. It's not a bad deal for illegal immigrants, either, who earn far more than they ever would have back home. A "drywallero" makes a lot more in Houston than in Honduras. So, we have to build the wall.

Walls are going up all over the world, even if Republican majorities in Congress won't really fight for them. Democrats tell us walls are racist. As President Trump reminds them, "We don't build walls because we hate the people on the outside. We do it because we love the people on the inside."

In the Third World nations the Democrats want to send more of your money to, you see how often walls are going up around homes. Some nations—such as Israel and Hungary—put walls around their borders. But to build a wall you need the will. Americans clearly have it more than their bought-off government does. The success of consumer products like Ring or caller ID prove that Americans want to know who is at their door wanting in, or on their phone seeking access. However high we build the wall, it won't be high enough to stop someone who overstays a visa, but we can stop new interlopers.

Walls must go up around some of our concepts, too. Citizenship should be one such concept. Birthright citizenship-by-fraud should not be allowed into the legal lexicon in America if we really love and cherish her as much as we should.

Nor is birthright citizenship recognized in many other places. Our left-wing courts often draw inspiration from foreign powers seeking to import foreign concepts into our law. And yet they are quite cautious about drawing lessons from abroad when it comes to birthright citizenship policies. It's easy to see why. Only thirty countries out of nearly two hundred practice birthright citizenship, Michael Anton notes. Fully 6.8 billion of the world's people live in regimes that bar birthright citizenship. Are they all racists and nativists too? Or do they cherish what they have more than we do?

All of our enemies want their money here and that's because we have integrity. You have to have integrity to have a country. You have to know who is coming and going and how often. Banks implemented Know Your Customer laws to stop money laundering by criminals. Employers need better technological tools to help make sure they aren't unwittingly employing illegal aliens. Do we not have a right to know who is in our home? If a man's home is his castle, does he not deserve to build a moat around it? Do he and his neighbors on Neighborly or the Neighborhood Watch not have a right to defend their homes? We can't have white picket fences if we can't trust our neighbors not to invade by climbing over them.

For most Americans, these issues are obvious, but not for our business elite. Let's explain the issue in terms that they can understand. If you and I started a company together and I suddenly added another class of shareholders, you'd rightly sue me for breaching our agreement. The elite have an obligation to protect the workers who we already have and are patriotically obligated to serve. To be a public servant, you must actually serve the public. To be a business leader, you have to lead. Maybe Mitt Romney is right, and corporations are in fact people. You should then be asking not what your country can do for your corporation but what your corporation can do for America.

But isn't America a nation of immigrants?

America is a nation of settlers who have restricted and permitted immigration when it suited our interests. Globalization has reduced the size of our world while simultaneously increasing its complexity. In 2020 and beyond, our immigration policy should not be based on a poem, and nor should it look and feel like a

Ponzi scheme. And no, illegal immigration is not an "act of love" as Jeb Bush put it, but of breaking and entering. Unlawful entry is a crime. In the best of scenarios, we hope that the breaking of our laws stops after getting here illegally, but all too often it doesn't. I've looked into the tear-filled eyes of Angel Mothers who lost children to violent illegals. The mere existence of the category Angel Mothers is living evidence of our failure. President Trump was right when he came down that escalator. They aren't sending their best—but they are taking ours.

There's been plenty of romanticism about the Ellis Island chapter in American history, but we are a fundamentally different country now, and those years were hardly the most stable in our history. There were anarchist bombings, organized crime, riots, machine bosses, and buying off of politicians and elections. Haven't you seen *Boardwalk Empire*? *Gangs of New York*? The numbers of those still coming are enormous—millions every year, some legally, some illegally. It makes little sense to import a low-skilled labor force before the robots automate our jobs.

Indeed, immigration and technology are always in tension. More immigration logically leads to less innovation. The higher the wage the better the market signal for entrepreneurs to build the next labor-saving robot. We oftentimes hear the phrase "jobs Americans just won't do" used by immigration boosters, but I've yet to hear of a robot who stole research for his overlords in the Communist Robot Empire.

Productivity gains usually come from "eating people" (that is, eliminating their jobs), as tech columnist Andy Kessler puts it, and software is eating the world, as tech investor Marc Andreessen puts it. Let us work to make sure that process doesn't eat us whole. How can we have an honest conversation about raising minimum wages for workers when we cannot even ensure that we have a legal workforce with an impenetrable E-Verify system?

Conservative immigration restrictionists all too often tell business owners to simply raise wages, but raising wages isn't the only solution. Who wants to pick lettuce at any price? The federal government is well aware of which industries employ the most illegal aliens. We should use the stick of federal enforcement but also the carrots of research and tax credits to empower employers to automate whatever illegal immigrant jobs they can. Illegal aliens can't take jobs that robots are already doing. We might even learn from our Japanese and Australian friends, who provide businesses with incentives to do just that.

There are, of course, some jobs that do require seasonal immigrant workers. There, we can follow our friends in South Korea and hold back a portion of their wages, giving them back once they've left the country.

ICE spent $3.2 billion to identify, arrest, detain, and remove illegal immigrants in 2016—the latest figures available before the mad rush on the border—while the cost of illegal immigration to our country is more than $100 billion annually, according to the Federation for American Immigration Reform (FAIR)—more than $6 billion just for the two million illegal aliens in Florida! Californians pay $23 billion for the more than six million illegal immigrants there and their children, while Texans pay more than $11 billion for the four million in the Lone Star State.

It also costs the taxpayers more than $15,000 to deport each illegal alien. The Democrats want to "abolish ICE." The corporatist Republicans want to ignore ICE. I want to enhance ICE and give it the latest tech—while singing, "ICE, ICE, baby"!

I kid, but I am never more serious than when I am joking. After all, as the Left tries to smear those of us with America First immigration views as grievance racists, we should be joyous about protecting our countrymen. It is a worthy and noble cause. Don't let anyone tell you different in America.

Reagan wanted to tear down the Berlin Wall, while George H. W. Bush wanted "a thousand points of light," whatever that means. Bill Clinton wanted to build a bridge to the future, and Barack Obama told us which direction the moral arc of the universe bent (really). Donald Trump wants to build a wall to protect and secure our southern border, and over 200 miles are already complete. And once we have built that wall, I want to man the gates.

There will be times when those gates can swing open, but they must always be closed to those who do not wish to be a part of our experiment in self-government, rooted in self-reliance. Those who do not want to partake of the American spirit ought not to settle in America, and we should never let them set foot here. Give us only those yearning to be free—and willing to fight for that freedom, as hard as those who built the country they have found worthy of joining.

There is no alternative, no country to run to, should America fail.

CHAPTER TWELVE

BIG TECH HATES AMERICA

January 2018
Capitol Hill Club.

AMERICA'S YOUNGEST SELF-MADE BOY BILLIONAIRE SAT ACROSS from me wearing flip-flops and a Hawaiian shirt—in January. As we sipped diet sodas, I sensed my congressional colleagues were reporting my plus-one to the Capitol Hill Club dress code committee.

I considered myself lucky, though. Time with the strange and brilliant is something I relish. In the world of Big Tech, you don't fit in if you are not ready to surrender everything you believe to the Woketopia, the paradise of those purportedly more politically aware than the rest of us.

But Woketopia has its dissidents—the real resistance—who seek to warn America before it is too late, even as they build the stuff of miracles. Palmer Luckey is like a free-internet Paul Revere. He was there to tell me the British are coming!

Palmer spoke in headlines—animated, excited about matters great and technical. The community college dropout founded his virtual reality company Oculus in his trailer and sold it to Facebook for a "couple billion dollars" in what was then the fastest acquisition in Silicon Valley history. Palmer dedicates 1 percent of his net worth annually to acquiring some astoundingly nerdy toys: Missile silos? Check. Submarines? Check. Buying ships from the navy? Check. Black Hawk helicopters? Check, check, check. If it's weird and cool and colorably legal, Palmer's got it. He's a legend in Japan—because of course he is.

Palmer had an urgent message: Big Tech seeks to dominate what we say and think and therefore how we act. They must be stopped. Palmer and I both know people who Big Tech has disappeared because of their heretical politics. I've seen the tech companies conduct elaborate opposition research projects against their critics. Six eBay executives and employees were even indicted for allegedly sending threats, including a bloody pig mask and books about how to survive the loss of a spouse, to a married couple who criticized them in an e-newsletter. Vicious! The innovators should know that disruption always wins in the end, though. America needs the nerds to keep its edge. What happens when Big Tech deletes its own conservatives? How many of them have been deleted already? Could a reboot to our technical-political thinking bring them back?

The Capitol Hill Club is the sort of stodgy place where lobbyists and politicians, dressed in their best, did their worst, often at America's expense. The "Club" is where you imagine conversations in smoke-filled rooms that determine America's fate take place—just without the smoking because, as you know, Washington kicked the smoking habit once Speaker John Boehner got run out of town. They're addicted to something far more dangerous now—power and money.

Neither Palmer nor I, the third-youngest elected congressman, belonged here among the dad ties and old man cologne. I avoid the place as much as I can.

Palmer positively bounced with the energy of his middle twenties as if everything were possible because for him, everything was. He had just founded another company—Anduril, "Flame of the West"—aimed squarely at building the (digital) wall that President Trump had campaigned on, using a surveillance array and AI instead of just concrete and steel. Early results from the digital wall experiment have been encouraging. Nerds like Palmer seem to summon the future and bring it forth. I dig it.

And yet when it came to the circumstances surrounding his untimely departure from Facebook, Palmer grew quiet before growing intense, urgent, and triggered.

Palmer's NDA barred him from talking to anyone but a government officer about it. Good thing he was in luck. I ask questions for a living, often of people who don't want to answer them. And Palmer had a story to tell.

"Mark Zuckerberg fired me from the company I created, for supporting Trump."

At first, it sounded disgruntled and impossible to prove. It turns out Palmer kept the receipts, and my jaw damn near hit the '70s-style carpet when he showed me the messages. Facebook absolutely fired one of America's great geniuses for backing Donald Trump. They even forced Palmer to issue a statement that they drafted and pretended was his own. There was no grey area in this fight. Zuckerberg was freaking out that an inventor and major shareholder had the audacity to back the ultimate winner. When he was brought before Congress, the android-like Zuckerberg was prepared for every question save one: "Why was Palmer Luckey fired?" His answer was perjury. He would be prosecuted if Palmer gave his evidence to the Senate or the Department of Justice.

Palmer also showed me a Facebook post he had written in 2012 encouraging Donald Trump to run for president. Palmer had even used the lessons he'd learned from *The Art of the Deal* to build his companies. (Palmer's whole story was later recounted in a best-selling book, *The History of the Future*, and in the *Wall Street Journal*.)

It's no secret that Silicon Valley is extremely, almost mono-maniacally left-wing. Palmer had been forced by one of the most powerful companies in the world to vote the way they wanted. He has since become a major donor to the Republican Party, including, in the spirit of full disclosure, to me.

But regardless, what happened to Palmer struck me as totally wrong. Worse yet, I was to learn that Palmer wasn't alone. Silicon Valley won't stop until we all think the same way—or else.

If Silicon Valley would do this to billionaires and their own colleagues, what would they do to the rest of us? If they could disappear the wunderkind who let us see a virtual reality, how easy is it to erase you and me?

More importantly, who would stop them?

The sometimes less-than-social network of Big Tech conservatives includes some of America's brightest minds and most-needed voices. It is truly a secret society, but I had been inducted. They had waited in vain for a politician who understands what we are up against. Believing I could be helpful in the fight against Silicon Valley, I was soon introduced to its most famous architect-turned-dissident: Peter Thiel.

I have become friendly with this PayPal cofounder and Facebook first investor. We have had breakfast at his home in L.A., lunch on Capitol Hill, and cocktails in the Big Apple. Peter once rolled out of bed in his home, high up in the West Hollywood hills, to greet me wearing nothing but his underwear and a nightshirt.

Weird, but OK! I have never met Peter in the Bay Area. There's a reason: he travels.

"Wherever there's a major shift in the American landscape in the past half-decade—be it political or cultural—there, somewhere on the donor list of the political campaign, or among the investors in the controversial technology, is Peter Thiel," writes *City Journal*. Peter's so involved that they call his clique the "PayPal Mafia." His investments include Airbnb, LinkedIn, and Elon Musk's SpaceX. Indeed, Thiel is the don of the PayPal Mafia—there's scarcely a major tech company that Peter hasn't founded or backed—and yet he left it all behind.

Why?

One of the least contrarian things Peter has ever done by normal American standards is back candidate Trump, but for that he has been made to pay a steep social price—I call it the Trump Tax, and it is especially steep in the tech world. Protestors chanted outside his home. Entrepreneurs refused to take his venture firm's money (or at least made a show of doing it reluctantly). He was a pariah and yet it turned out he was a prophet. The brilliant among us often are. And Peter is the most brilliant man I've ever met. We need him back on the Trump team ASAP.

Reed Hastings, Netflix CEO and then Thiel's fellow Facebook board member, had written him an email telling him that he was going to give him a bad performance review—not because Peter was bad on the board but for backing Trump and "showing seriously poor judgment." Naughty, naughty, Peter!

Peter didn't back down. He gave an electric Republican Convention speech in 2016 and received a standing ovation when he declared, "I'm proud to be gay. I am proud to be a Republican. But most of all I'm proud to be an American!" When Donald Trump got in trouble over his old "locker room talk" tape for his bawdy comments, many fair-weather Republicans deserted him.

Not so Peter. He doubled down with a donation and gave a great speech making the unafraid case for Trumpism and America First when it was most needed.

One of Peter's key insights is that because it effectively costs nothing to distribute the latest and greatest software, your company can get to scale very quickly and literally take over the world. If you have a really good idea, you really can get it everywhere. That's when the network effects really kick in. Thiel and his co-author Blake Masters write about that tendency in *Zero to One: Notes on Startups, or How to Build the Future*:

> *Monopolies deserve their bad reputation—but only in a world where nothing changes…. In a static world, a monopolist is just a rent collector. If you corner the market for something you can jack up the price…but the world we live in is dynamic: it's possible to invent new and better things. Creative monopolists give customers more choices by adding entirely new categories of abundance to the world. Creative monopolies aren't just good for the rest of society; they're powerful engines for making it better.*

And yet the bigger the monopolists get, the less creative they seem to be. It's impossible to invent new and better things if you can't openly collaborate about what needs to be fixed or invented.

The tech companies spent the last ten years addicting people to their vices. LinkedIn cofounder Reid Hoffman bragged about how the best companies are those that celebrate the seven deadly sins. (Twitter is wrath, Instagram vanity, Uber Eats gluttony, Tinder lust, and so on.) In the long run, the wages of sin are death. But in the meantime, tech has enjoyed wages of a different sort as Silicon Valley turns the most productive minds to the most wasteful of tasks—addicting people and turning them into mindless consumers.

"The best minds of my generation are thinking about how to make people click ads," noted former wunderkind Jeff Hammerbacher, a twenty-three-year-old math genius recruited to work for Facebook. "This sucks," he pronounced. And yet it's very rational to go work for Facebook.

In politics, we treat monopolies differently because of their overwhelming and corrosive effects on the public square and marketplace. We recognize that monopolies are bad not just for the public but also for those holding the monopoly. They do little to encourage innovation; they use their largesse to buy off competitors. Note, for example, how America's tech monopolists are partnering and buying companies with India's. Sure, Indian monopolies were built with graft and ours with grit, but are we really so confident that they won't end up behaving the same way in the end?

Past thinkers on monopoly, including Judge Robert Bork, argued that monopolies need not be bad for consumers, but we are not a nation of consumers. We are a nation of free citizens. Not everything that has a price can be put into dollars and cents. There is a high price for free things. We should always be embarrassed by monopolies—and not make excuses for them. They should have to explain themselves to us, and to the extent that they are necessary, they should behave in ways that are in the national interest. While businessmen may seek to be monopolies, statesmen seek to bust them.

This trust-busting must be done when a monopoly ventures into those areas that intersect with the public discourse. We cannot tolerate an enforced private monopoly in public opinion; we must be free to disagree not because we know all the answers but because we know so few. Information makes us free. And so, too, does open debate.

"Public sentiment is everything," said Abraham Lincoln during one of his famous debates with Stephen A. Douglas. "With public sentiment, nothing can fail; without it nothing can succeed. Consequently he who molds public sentiment, goes deeper than he who enacts statues or pronounces decisions. He makes statutes and decisions possible or impossible to be executed." Lincoln would have dominated cable news.

What about he who codes to suppress public sentiment? I fear we are already finding out.

THE MAJOR TECH COMPANIES—FACEBOOK, TWITTER, AMAZON, Google, YouTube—make it impossible for tech's best minds to help make America great again if they ever want to work in technology. Like all people playing intimidation games, these companies make an example of the weak.

Software engineer James Damore was fired from Google for pointing out well-established personality research between the sexes. Kevin Cernekee was also fired from Google. He warned on Tucker Carlson's show that he, along with other conservatives, had been harassed and bullied and added to an internal political blacklist. In America you should be fired for being bad at your job—not your "bad views." No wonder Elon Musk calls it "Sanctimonious Valley." We wanted flying cars, but we got Communistic struggle sessions.

Cernekee raised the problem to the Google human resources department and eventually the California and federal labor boards. He was ignored. He told the country about the censorship on national TV, but still our conservative leaders are "monitoring" the situation—and doing nothing to fix it.

Absolute power corrupts absolutely, and tech increasingly has absolute power over what we see, feel, and hear. They've bought off most of our politicians, Republican and Democrat alike.

In Washington, corruption is often a family affair. When they can't buy a congressman, they oftentimes buy the kids or spouse. A lot of members have adult kids working for the tech companies, including Senate Minority Leader Chuck Schumer, whose daughter Alison works as project manager for Facebook. Facebook has donated hundreds of thousands to and through Chuck Schumer, who worked with the company to stop regulation.

Bobby Goodlatte is a left-wing venture capitalist who praised the FBI agents who worked to overthrow the results of the 2016 election, calling Peter Strzok "a patriot." Bobby's father—Congressman Bob Goodlatte of Virginia—stopped meaningful tech regulation when Republicans were in the majority. That wasn't good enough for his son, who endorsed and raised $40,000 for the Democrat seeking to replace his own dad in Congress.

"The way you raise money on the Judiciary is by playing the tech companies and the content publishers against each other," Chairman Goodlatte told me in my first year. How degrading.

Former UN ambassador Nikki Haley (R-Establishment) seems resigned to defeat in the battle against Big Tech. Or is her acceptance of the status quo an obvious signal she is on their side? Her tweet was like a white flag of surrender: "Censorship by tech companies, esp censorship of conservative opinions, violates the spirit of the law & the 1st Amendment. But more regulation would go too far in the other direction, putting bureaucrats & lawyers in control of what gets said online. Either way, free speech loses." Either way free speech loses? Not exactly the talk of winners. We should fight like hell to vindicate the rights of all Americans. Losing should not be an option, much less a strategy.

With "leaders" like this, we can be forgiven for thinking we might never be able to stop the tech companies from undermining our elections.

And yet stories continue to get out about the censorship of American voices and about harassment. What began as a conspiracy theory has now reached the desk of the president of the United States. He promises reforms, and I've introduced them along with Sen. Josh Hawley. He has promised executive action, and I'm going to advise him on how to deliver it.

To fix our tech companies, we must bear witness to their flaws. The truth always triumphs against tyranny, even if it takes a while for most of us to notice there's a battle going on. Eventually, though, we do. There is no algorithm that can break the human will to do the right thing. And so there have been brave whistleblowers who have detailed how Facebook and Twitter and Google and Pinterest suppress conservative content with impunity and without apology.

We must be courageous enough to encourage these brave voices to guide us and to expose what's truly rotten at these #AmericaLast companies. All technology means is doing more with less. You can sometimes have more tyranny at a cheaper price. If we are entering a networked world, denying someone access to that network constitutes a kind of maliciousness we should oppose. Ever since the ancient world, we had two punishments—death and banishment. It's easier to ban your opponents than to debate them.

Software is eating the world, prominent VC and Facebook board member Marc Andreessen once said. And it is eating our political discourse whole.

Your wealth is a function of your intelligence, your capacity for risk, and network social media bans are a kind of taking, no less personally destructive than taking property. Do we make America great again by banning people with bad politics from Uber or DoorDash or Instacart? Why again do we allow the tech or for that matter banking companies to work with fraudulent hate groups like the Southern Poverty Law Center to determine who can use their products? Does the heart of a tyrant beat in the heart of every Woketopian? Are they all secretly building the Chinese social credit score system to turn us all into their captive Uighurs?

Naivete has made us terribly vulnerable. Google partnered with the Chinese Communist military to build artificial intelligence—but not the U.S. military. More than 1,600 Google employees petitioned CEO Sundar Pichai to deny cops basic email services. The woke Left wants the cops to show up when they are under attack, but heaven forbid they have a right to access the basic digital necessities. Twitter hired a Chinese Communist Party-linked A.I. expert who wanted to hide "secret" weapons contracts.

We must make our tech sector love America before our tech overlords take us over. Here, policy can be our guide.

Big Tech should be required to provide transparency to validate the neutrality of its platform. Valid explanations should accompany all takedowns and suspensions. It was embarrassing when Jack Dorsey didn't even know why users were suspended. Individual users should be able to appeal, be told exactly where they went out of bounds (quotes, timestamp) and exactly what policy guidelines they violated. The big platforms should also be required to publish aggregate data on takedowns/suspensions. Maybe also have an independent board of review. It should be hard to comply with the conditions justifying bans so that they'll censor less.

We need a culture of free speech, and large or market-dominant communication platforms need to serve the public interest rather than their own whims. The big players need to be regulated as common carriers.

Big Tech needs to stop hurting the little guy. Sure, they need to remove spammers, scams, and child porn, but their algorithmic tools can't be allowed to censor sociopolitical ideas, constitutionally protected hate speech, or everything deemed "misinformation." Twitter has now made it so that their employees can work from anywhere. They should do what they can to make sure that that army of employees is representative of society as a whole, not just a narrow group of Silicon Valley woketopians.

Ban foreign companies like TikTok that are little more than data collection operations. We must ban certain Chinese organizations from operating in our country, just as they have with ours. Why do we allow the Chinese state to buy access to genetics companies like 23andMe or Complete Genomics anyway?

Don't set sweeping public policy targeting FAANG (Facebook, Amazon, Apple, Netflix, and Google) that winds up screwing upstarts, though. Making large and small companies play by the same rules will always favor the large companies.

Major operating system vendors need to offer a level playing field and encourage third-party innovation. They need to let third-party developers replace their built-in apps and let users replace their OS with modified versions on the hardware they own. App store curation shouldn't exclude software that the OS finds distasteful.

Politics and tech need not be in an antagonistic conflict. Whatever necessary tech disruption occurs should ultimately make America great and not just enrich a few in tony zip codes. Ask not what America can do for your tech company but what your tech company can do for America.

CHAPTER THIRTEEN

REVENGE PORN CHIVALRY

October 27, 2019
World Series Game 5. Presidential Sky Box.
Washington Nationals Stadium.

"You're dating her, aren't you?"

I was not.

"No, Mr. President. But chivalry is not dead. And I'm a sucker for a damsel in distress. Besides, we all fall short of perfection in our personal lives. That doesn't mean she should be getting bullied like this."

(Melania nodded in approval.)

The president pointed to then-congressman Mark Meadows, his best beltway buddy, and then back at me.

"He's dating her. Totally dating her. And he won't even admit it to his favorite president."

I have never dated *that* congresswoman, Katie Hill. Katie came to Washington a term after me, in the 2018 "blue wave," but with much more initial acclaim. She was a rising star in the new Democratic majority before she even took the oath. Hot, young, and blonde. Openly bisexual. From donor-rich California. She beat a multi-term Republican. A documentary movie chronicled her upstart millennial campaign. Well…most of it.

Katie and her husband Kenny were having sex with a young female campaign staffer. Apparently that arrangement is called a throuple—a festive label for sure. It's weird, but in my experience, very normal-looking relationships can inflict just as much pain and resentment as the strange ones. If folks aren't getting hurt any more than usual, I'm not a judger. Different strokes for different folks. Live and let live. Besides, I have plenty to work on to be a better partner in my own relationships before judging the choices others make in theirs.

All good throuples come to an end, apparently. Who knew that wasn't the most stable of affairs? This one ended with now-estranged Kenny releasing Congresswoman Hill's naked pics online. Bongs, questionable tattoos, and scenes with Katie and her staffer without clothes dripped out over several days.

I have already laid out my rules against sleeping with staffers. But technically there is no congressional rule against sleeping with *campaign* staff. Maybe there should be. Though, more than a few congressmen have ended up marrying their campaign workers. My predecessor Joe Scarborough did. Ex-Mrs. Scarborough #2—after the intern stuff, before the co-host stuff. All's fair in love and war and MSNBC.

Releasing revenge porn is a crime and it should be. If two people (or, given the example, maybe more) share photos in the confines of a relationship, society shouldn't judge the object of the image as harshly as we judge the betraying releaser. Only a bully violates trust for spite and sport. And I have never tolerated bullies. My dad taught me to stand up to them. No matter the trouble I found myself in during school, if I was pushing back against a bully, all was absolved at home.

Sometimes home can be the scene of the crime. Katie's mean husband was victimizing her—our colleague. Adding to the very real photos were very false claims that Katie was also sleeping with her congressional staff (apparently this time without Kenny). Katie and everyone who worked with her in the House of Representatives denied that she was. Who knows? Who cares? Nobody complained. But as Professor Alan Dershowitz points out, too often we accept Guilt by Accusation, especially if the details are salacious and tribal.

Congress treated a female member expressing her sexuality worse than the man exploiting her because of it. It wasn't our best hour fighting the Man.

If you are a liberal, California Democrat the only thing potentially worse than having nobody defend you is having only Matt Gaetz defend you. But where was the sisterhood of the traveling pantsuit?!

Did the woke women of the new Democratic majority stand up for Katie? Did the squad don pink hats and organize protests? Did it occur to them that an abusive man was ruining the life of a human being we worked with who broke no rule and was the subject of no complaint?

One hundred and two women serve in the House—more than ever before in America's history. But not one initially stood up for Katie. #ImWithHer was quickly converted to #ShesOnHerOwn. I had Katie's back in hours. The few who ever spoke up took days and weeks as their wet fingers tested the political winds. It takes these feminists-in-name-only less political courage to smear President Trump than to stand up for one of their own against a real monster.

If the Democrats were too gutless to defend Katie, the Republicans were all too happy to see an opponent embarrassed—maybe even forced to resign. Could we retake the seat? Get excited! None of us are at our best when singularly focused on the zero-sum nature of power in Washington. (We did end up winning the seat. More on that in a moment.)

Tribalism makes us blind and careless. It reduces us from being our best selves and stops us from living our best lives. I don't believe in defending every Republican just because they are a Republican. Ask senator Richard Burr, whom I roasted for selling off stocks during the coronavirus pandemic as he lied to America publicly. He's now a *former* chairman and will never win an election again. He may even go to prison given the current FBI investigation of his conduct. If he cheated and lied to the country for personal gain, he should.

I also won't attack Democrats just because they are Democrats. As the son of a mother confined to a wheelchair most of my life, I hate when people pick on the vulnerable and weak. I stand up for those who can't stand up for themselves. I believe in civil rights for the gay, the trans, the unborn, and our animal friends. It's why I support laws that crack down on those who abuse defenseless animals. It's why I'm the only Republican co-sponsor of the FAIR Act to stop mandatory arbitration in employment claims. Sexual harassers shouldn't get to pick their own juries in advance.

"Who among us would look perfect if every ex leaked every photo or text? Katie isn't being investigated by Ethics or maligned because she hurt anyone—it is because she is different," I tweeted.

I wasn't done.

"Congress should write a budget before we play 'bedroom police' or allow an ex to illegally humiliate our colleague for being different. Key fact: Not a whiff of a complaint from anyone who has worked for Congresswoman Hill. Just an angry ex releasing revenge porn. Sad!"

My very young staff all have alerts on their phones for my tweets. My Chief of Staff Jillian Lane-Wyant, Operations Director Alison Thomas, and Communications Director Luke Ball are the very best at what they do on Capitol Hill. They prepare, scheme, and strategize constantly. I do not lower their blood pressure. "If something embarrassing came out about you, she'd never have your back. Why are you doing this?! Republican congressmen don't defend Democrats in sex scandals, boss!" Ah, youthful idealism.

"Why Is Matt Gaetz Defending Katie Hill?" asked *Mother Jones*, a liberal oppo research outfit masquerading as a news organization. They couldn't figure it out. Maybe I had nudes. I don't. At least I hope not. But who really knows anymore? Could it just be a crass political play for young voters? Aren't we supposed to want young people to vote? Was I gay? If I am, I'm terrible at it. Not that there is anything wrong with it.

In boomer Congress the millennial notion that we've all made mistakes—the pictures are everywhere—and we don't get too worked up about it, is totally alien. My mug shot from an arrest twelve years ago is online. So what? Some people share nudes. Big deal. Do we really care? The president is friends with Kim Kardashian, and we all know how she became famous. Kardashian is now using her fame to help others. Good for her. We millennials contain multitudes.

As millennials, we were handed phones with video cameras at the most hormonal stage of life and we document every transgression. Who needs the deep state when you have an Instagram history of every slutty Halloween costume? What did you think we were going to do? What would we know of our parents and their worst choices if they had been boomeranging through Woodstock naked and throwing the sexual revolution of the '70s on TikTok?

We can't see them drop acid on Snapchat though they don't stop chatting about how great it was to break all the rules that they expect us to follow in technicolor. We learned of our parents' youth through grainy family photos in Sunday's best. Our children will digitally harvest HD images of the body paint we wore to Coachella. The permanent record they scoffed at is something we live with. Our digital identity is our real identity and vice versa for better and oftentimes for worse.

We need more weirdos in Congress—more MIT geniuses like Rep. Thomas Massie and more risk-takers like Rep. Louie Gohmert of Texas, who abandoned the black robe of the judiciary for the fray of Congress. We need the freak flags to fly at full—not half-mast. The place is far too boring because it is filled with old bores.

Rep. Charlie Wilson plotted the demise of the Soviet Union amid hookers and blow in a hot tub. Where are all the badasses we were promised?

Only fools would expect this boring batch of octogenarians and septuagenarians to solve our most serious crises when they are themselves on their way to checking out of the hotel of life.

The budget crisis, climate change, Big Tech bias, immigration, or any number of other generational issues require the focus and attention of those who will deal with these crises and their aftermath. The young have perspectives the old do not.

It gives us a chance to be more real, more, yes, representative, if we seize it. Everyone just needs to stop clutching their pearls long enough to evolve. President Trump evolved. So should we.

May 16, 2020
Camp David. Movie theater, watching Tora! Tora! Tora!

"My Kevin is a genius! He said we'd be the first to flip a California seat from blue to red in recent history. We did it!"

McCarthy went all in and won back Katie Hill's seat in a special election with fantastic candidate recruitment and millions upon millions of dollars. Sex had cost the Democrats power. Or at least a House seat. Or was it momentum? Perhaps a sign of good things to come in the 2020 election? I guess we'll see.

"Hey, Gaetz." I was sitting behind the president during the movie. He talks the whole time and doesn't miss a line. "That thing you did for the girl with the naked pictures. That was a good thing. You were right to do that."

The president is at his best when he is being magnanimous. But I still couldn't convince him I never dated her.

CHAPTER FOURTEEN

UNCANCELED

The radical Left of the '90s and '00s wanted the power to control our lives with government. They essentially won on all fronts.

I wrote most of this book under a coronavirus lockdown strong enough to strangle small businesses to death, but our ailments began much earlier. When Republicans lost elections, government took over health care and the economy. Things weren't any better when we won. George W. Bush grew government, creating new federal agencies and inventing new authorities to spy on us. After the reign of "43," now treated as a beloved elder statesman, government was strong enough to have secret courts approve any desired political interference based on fabricated or altered evidence. "Compassionate conservatism" sure was nosy.

Winning against some of our party's boring standard-bearers—Bush, Romney, McCain—hasn't satiated the Left's thirst for power. The Republican losers of yesteryear had fortitude but not electoral success. Perhaps they were wonderful men, some like Sen. McCain even great men, but they were losers all the same, Romney and McCain at the ballot box, Bush in the annals of history. Appeasement is always and everywhere a weak strategy. We were promised "peace through strength," but we got war without winning.

The conflict that matters most, though, is domestic, and the political struggle here can be just as vicious. Ivanka Trump can't give a speech at Wichita State to empower women and inspire a modern workforce thanks to leftist pressure there. I don't want to live in a world too woke for Ivanka. First they came for the nerds; then they came for the hotties. This cannot stand.

The Left wasn't satisfied feasting on the political carcasses of Republican losers and wimps. They've grown hungrier. Today, the woke Left wants to control what we see, hear, and say so they can program what we think. Woketopia achieved! America defeated. CHAZ proliferated and widely adopted.

If we consider our enslavement by political correctness "small stuff we can sweat," if we tell ourselves to be still as uncomfortable ideas around us are canceled, the story of America is finished. No other issue we examine in this book will matter, because the future will belong to the controllers forever and ever. Political correctness and its Big Tech hall monitors are more dangerous than any South American caravan or Middle Eastern mullah. If we lose, it will be the only fight that mattered. If we win, every future debate is a fair one and therefore we are the favorite to win them.

You never know when the mob will come for you—or for the voices that stir your American First ambitions. You must always be ready. The mob is always waiting for its chance to take your scalp. They are the witch-hunters who never want to run out of witches. Tweet the wrong thing and you're erased, just like that. But preemptively give up the arena—the public square—and it will be like you never existed to begin with. Invisible.

Why bother with politics, why bother with anything, if nobody hears what you say or argues for a better nation? What if

Reagan had been banned from TV? Or Obama from the internet? Or Trump from Twitter? As each of those communications revolutions occurred, those of us who wanted to partake and might have an unpopular view had the element of surprise. Now, though, we have targets on our back—every deplorable among us. That which our enemies could not achieve through election, they now seek to do through algorithm. It's all about shutting us up. Well, I aim to misbehave. I was promised we would win so much we'd get tired of winning, and I'm not yet the least bit gassed.

Bill Clinton's Democrats of the '90s would "Mediscare" old people—especially in my beloved Florida—to win elections, making people think they'd be left without doctors. Those politicians, tactics, and targets may be fading away, though. Today's woke Left is after the young, the future. It seeks to dominate them with debt and diminished expectations—but most of all by narrowing their intellectual horizons.

Millennials and zoomers experience the world principally through their phones. Control what they see, and you control their destiny—and ultimately all of ours. What sorts of things will trend on that phone? What ideas will be permitted? What arguments will be suppressed, curated, or promoted? Meme magic (manipulations through catchy ideas) is real, and there are magicians among us, with quite a few practicing the dark arts.

LIKE THE PRESIDENT, I USE TWITTER TO GO DIRECTLY TO THE people. And like the president, my successful use of technology angers my political opponents, precisely because I am so effective at it. They'd like to think that they alone control the conversation because they control the narrative. They tilt the field of debate in their favor. All tech companies go through an evolution: liberation, then corporate control, then government control, and ultimately woke left-wing despotism. Absolute power corrupts absolutely, and centralized power makes controlling thought easier. Those who own the platform think they own the content—and therefore they have no need to debate; they simply bid ideas they dislike adieu. Shaming and shadowbanning are easier than winning the votes of real Americans, they've learned.

They really do shadowban the arguments they don't want people to see—like when Twitter got busted by Vice News for shadowbanning the four members of Congress most aggressively defending Trump: Meadows, Nunes, Jordan, and Gaetz.

We are "too dangerous," they tell us. But real danger befalls a people managed and programmed by prevailing thinking at Manhattan dinner parties or Silicon Valley gender-intersection-ality seminars. The Left treats us as children. We are so weak that we cannot confront the strange, uncomfortable, and even horrid thoughts expressed in a free society, they say with their demands for censorship. But the First Amendment doesn't exist only to protect pleasant speech. Sometimes we necessarily are all unpleasant—especially in politics.

Politics is inherently divisive. Congressmen used to cane each other. Roman senators stabbed Caesar. Cuban representa-tives break into fistfights in the Florida legislature every few years. Sure, we should all aspire to the most austere of political engage-ment. And yet when we fall short, now the digital death penalty is imposed, and it's both prosecuted and enforced by faceless cogs who we will never meet. It is a cold regime. There is no appeal. It is un-American to be deprived of the opportunity to face your accuser. It is positively antihuman.

For the most part, the prison wardens of Woketopia are right that Republicans don't know how to communicate, so censoring them isn't really necessary. Few bother to seize the narrative. Instead, they sacrifice boldness at the altar of fear. To avoid Twitter Jail, they won't commit the crime of independent thought or provocative speech—assuming of course they have either to offer. But then, it's downright shocking how ineffectual most Republicans are. The court of last resort isn't the Supreme Court but the court of public opinion. You should learn to joust and engage in combat if you ever expect to win. The public loves a champion and will tolerate you getting knocked off the horse and muddy if you get right back up and get back to it.

"We ain't one-at-a-timin' here, we're mass communicating!" to borrow a line from one of my favorite movies, *O Brother, Where Art Thou?* When we're tweeting nowadays, we're governing and doing so at the speed of thought. We wanted flying cars, but we got 140 and now 280 characters. I intend to make every one of them count. Leftism requires carefully laid plans because it needs to work so hard to sell the lies it is peddling. Twitter allows us to disrupt the cycle and to always keep them on their back foot, unsure of when and where we will hit them next.

Twitter also has many participants who, like all cults, do little thinking and much signaling. Sycophants will happily retweet whatever the cause du jour is, no matter how absurd. The more absurd the better. It doesn't matter if it's true. It only matters if it trends—just so long as the mob doesn't get them. The hashtag is not a program but a slogan, a sentiment. Their Woketopia will never be achieved, but that's kind of the point, isn't it? Cheap grace cheapens people and turns them into liars, pretending each new battle is the pivotal one. Really, they're just terrified their fellow social justice warriors will turn on them if they display a lack of zeal. Cowardice is contagious, and it too goes viral if you let it.

But then again, courage is contagious too. I won't surrender, not to the mob, not to the Chinese, and certainly not to the press. But everything in politics now is about trying to bring you to your knees. Once you are on your knees, you never get to stand tall again. You're done. And everyone knows it.

Twitter "labeled" one of my tweets for "glorifying violence." I explicitly and frequently speak against political violence in America. What did I tweet? That following the designation of Antifa as a terrorist organization by the Department of Justice, I hoped we would hunt them down with all the vigor with which we prosecuted our War on Terror. The threat of Antifa is real and it is here.

Patrick Underwood was killed serving our country as a federal police officer in Oakland, California. Rioters shot him. He was fifty-three. Captain David Dorn had retired from the St. Louis Police Department but was willing to help his friend defend his small business from looters. It cost him his life. Both of these dead American heroes are black. As Project Veritas proved in an explosive video series showing an Antifa-insider-turned-informant, these people intend violence and death. The only way to give them what they want is to give them everything—your submission, your fortune, your children—up to and including your life.

My oath is to defend the Constitution against all enemies foreign and domestic, and I will keep my oath come what way— in the real world, and online. It is hard to cancel a congressman, though many try. Just ask former congressmen Steve King or Dana Rohrabacher. Fame is both weapon and shield. It makes you a target but also makes them have to work to get you. All political lives end in failure, in a sense, but some are spectacular. Better to be a spectacle than to end up having never said anything worth canceling because nobody was listening in the first place.

Federal law is quite clear about instigating mobs, at least in the *real* world. But the line between what is real and what is online keeps blurring. Online bullying is now a crime in most states. The consequences of an online politically correct mob can be almost as devastating as a real one. Social media has become the new public square, and every so often there's a digital firing squad. Like the executions of old, these "cancelations" have become a regular, even routine, occurrence. Mob-instigator Twitter even has the audacity to "fact-check" its targets against the claims of left-wing groups, including criminally fraudulent hate groups like the Southern Poverty Law Center.

When everyone is informing on themselves constantly by living so publicly thanks to social media, there's a lot of fodder for self-appointed opposition researchers. Who needs the CIA when my generation had drunk Facebooking? The KGB would have loved the technology we've made to spy on ourselves.

Writer Scott Adams promotes the twenty-year rule on ignoring past behavior and the forty-eight-hour rule for apologies and corrections. After those spans, move on. Time will only shorten these windows.

The pressure to conform has led to an increase in suicide as young people find it hard to measure up to the Instagram version of their lives. For the young, social life isn't mall life or sports life, it's internet life. We don't go out drinking on the weekends, but we do make sure every photo we have is perfect, just as we are not. There is a deep irony in Silicon Valley's nerds creating the ideal hotbed for bullying—social media—as if they decided to make the entire world feel the pain that they felt being stuffed in lockers. Have our tweets become the new social credit score before we even realized it?

There is a still-darker part of tech-enabled cancel culture. In theory, social media elevates the best ideas; in practice, it descends into recrimination, fake news, and foreign influence. Which drug treatment should we take to avoid the pandemic? Who knows. When everything is tribal and nothing is sacred, everything is a free-for-all, forever. Cancel culture targets the weak, the odd, the different—the very sorts of offbeat people we need to make the kinds of advances that made America great and will keep her that way. We talk often of safe spaces on our campuses, but we need a safe space for the truly odd among us, so long as they aren't hurtful.

President George H. W. Bush said upon seizing the GOP nomination in 1988, "I'm a quiet man.... I see the quiet people." Well, maybe I'm a weird man. I surely see the weird people. It is my view that the brilliant people in our society are often rare, precious, and strange. They sometimes don't get basic things right. But they can get complex things perfect. They are the real 1 percent who toil endlessly on the gadgets and gizmos that give us the advantages we need to advance humankind. Throughout history, many of the most brilliant have been profoundly unhappy—sometimes happy only when they are working on the sorts of problems that interest them and them alone.

Alan Turing—the father of modern computing—defeated Nazi Germany with a team he assembled based on their answers to crossword puzzles placed in newspapers. Turing happened to be gay, and he took his own life in shame. Turing and the greatest acting director of national intelligence in American history, Richard Grenell, prove that patriotism isn't lashed to bedroom dogmas.

But historical figures we now consider heroes were strange in ways that might now make them targets for the online mob, maybe even cancelation.

Sir Isaac Newton proclaimed he was proud to die a virgin. Bizarre! Tragic, even if you ask me. Howard Hughes revolutionized air travel and then became a bizarre recluse pissing in milk bottles. Cancel that weirdo! Put him on Zoloft and wheel him into the corner. We are now routinely told to wash our hands, but Ignaz Semmelweis was mocked, jailed, and killed for telling us to do just that. Yet he is revered by modern-day nerds for discovering germ theory. The brightest among us are often appreciated only after the rest of us catch up. Sometimes they even have to die first, like accused witches.

Exceptional oddities must be husbanded in the service of our country. We need America's Geek Squad to beat the rest of the world. They've done it in business. Why not politics? Is that their last frontier?

Canceling our nerds and misfits gives them little incentive to contribute. Most aren't motivated by money. Certainly, the ones I'll discuss later aren't. No wonder so many of them are trying to build rockets to leave us behind—or build web pages to find girls seeking expensive handbags. They're different. God love them, and especially forgive them. I sure have.

"YOU MUST FIRE YOUR LEGISLATIVE CORRESPONDENT," MY FATHER said. My father had never given me human resources advice before. We had served in the Florida Legislature together. At times we famously disagreed, but we always knew our unbreakable bond meant we had the rest of the Florida establishment surrounded. "Lots of people are calling me," he reported honestly, earnestly.

I barely knew my new legislative correspondent. I had intended to hire someone else for the position—someone I knew. But Devin Murphy asked if he could submit a writing sample to compete for any open job. It was brilliant prose, so he started three days later. He was paid $33,000 base salary and has opposed every salary increase he's earned over three years. A serious legislative office cannot pay its best people unfair wages, even if they would gladly accept them. Reluctantly he took the money—and then bought his subordinates suits because he believed in them, and in the mission.

The smart among us are motivated by being around beauty—and being around Firebrands. Excellence loves competent company.

When I assigned the objective to assemble legislative research on the corruption of Hillary Clinton, Devin partially crowdsourced it—on Reddit. Reddit was castigated as a white supremacy playground. Ironically, following the riots over the killing of George Floyd, Reddit's cofounder resigned from the board, demanding a black man replace him. If you can't beat the platform, you can at least try to outdo its virtue signaling.

I never considered firing Devin—not for a second. If my team makes mistakes, I want it to be because they are trying to learn too much, seek too many perspectives. Making the same mistakes repeatedly is one thing, but we seek to make bold, new, fresh, exciting mistakes and to learn from them. Fail fast! We aren't afraid of information—only incompetence. Laziness and acceptance of what passes for an acceptable status quo are more unacceptable to me than unorthodoxy is. Devin Murphy is a fantastic member of our team and now serves as my legislative director. He wasn't the last hiring risk I took.

The *American Conservative*'s Curt Mills put it plainly. I've made "some maverick personnel choices." Curt's report was accurate:

> Darren J. Beattie…was fired from the White House last summer to the consternation of many Trump loyalists. His transgression? Beattie spoke on the same panel as Peter Brimelow, an immigration restrictionist writer with deep ties to the American elite from his days as a financial journalist. Brimelow, who is most notably friends with Lawrence Kudlow, the White House economic point man and former CNBC anchor, has been frequently described as a white nationalist (Brimelow denies the charge). Beattie says he had never met Brimelow before that day. By hiring Beattie, Gaetz drew a line in the sand. Games of guilt by association have to stop. "Darren Beattie did nothing wrong," Gaetz told me.

I'm proud Darren has worked with our team. Not many PhDs serve Congress. We need more brilliant, strange minds. After all, our country was founded by them and will be maintained by them. The People's House gets what it pays for, which usually isn't much. I get briefings at 3:00 AM I didn't ask for, research from the corners of the internet some are scared to access, and talent from the places others wouldn't look. The best people must be inspired and honed, not just bought or rented. You can't afford them if they haven't already invested in you. Our movement deserves no less than dedicated patriots—and leaders who will admire those patriots' best and improve their worst. I'll never be too woke to forgive.

The media will never forgive me for bringing conservative investor Charles Johnson to President Trump's first State of the Union. I seek neither forgiveness nor permission from the Fake News.

I was supposed to bring my father. He had bronchitis and had to bail at the last minute. Word got out among the Florida Delegation that I had an available ticket. A colleague asked me to accommodate one of his supporters. It was Charles. We had only spent a few minutes together, but the dude is clearly brilliant and interesting, so I was happy to oblige. I'm a giver.

When the Daily Beast called asking whether I had invited Charles, it seemed routine—like they were checking who everyone's plus-one had been. I later learned that Charles had said some very terrible things, which today he deeply regrets and do not reflect the person he has grown into. Growth is a good thing for all of us. When they called him a Holocaust denier, I was ready to join the mob. Tar and feather him! Holocaust denial is not acceptable to me in any form. Charles even called me up and told me that he didn't have those views but was cool with me throwing him under the bus. He didn't want to hurt the mission, and he didn't want to hurt me. "Fuck 'em," he said, and he meant it. "You say whatever you've got to say, and know that I don't care because I'll know it isn't true. Denounce away." See what I mean about weird people?

Then I got a call from Alan Dershowitz, the de facto president of secular Jewish America and, as luck would have it, one of Charles's old bosses. Charles was an instigator, a provoker, Dershowitz said, but not an anti-Semite—far from it. Without seeking recognition, Charles was a donor to the Simon Wiesenthal Center, which hunts down Nazis and brings them to justice. He had invested in the dreams and inventions of diverse companies, including many led by Jews and immigrants. As a test of its censorship mores, he had posted absurd claims on Reddit. It was dumb, but should it cancel every past or future contribution he could make? Of course not.

I've needed second chances in life—and third and fourth chances in relationships. In the church where I worship, we pray for forgiveness and acknowledge our wretched flaws. I've begged at the altar for the absolution of mine. Someone died for our sins on Earth. At least some of them should be forgiven online.

When I told Jake Tapper live on CNN that Charles Johnson wasn't a Holocaust denier—that many prominent members of the Jewish community had assured me as much—some recoiled, but many learned I was right. My public service is enhanced because people like Charles, Darren Beattie, and Devin Murphy give me the best they have all the time, often without asking for anything other than that I be at my best. And I can look past the worst some have (falsely or fairly) been accused of doing. I know no one bats a thousand. I sure don't.

But the president did call me Mickey Mantle one time. Like Mantle, I'd rather be a legend than a never-was. Will there be strikeouts? You betcha. But anyone who has never gotten up to the plate isn't fit to judge the game, not from the bleachers.

The nerds are strange, sure, but I love them, and they love me. I admire what they can contribute despite their oddities. As I put it to Bill Maher when he falsely claimed I pick on nerds: I am the nerd! Not a whole lot of bullies were on the high school debate team, nor won the state's award for top nerd. I've done my time in debate camp and know of what I speak. Boring men don't make history. Most don't even make the debate team.

The measure of a great man is who he picks up, not who he pushes down. It takes more than fortitude. It takes character to remember the forgotten man and make him feel seen and to see more in himself. And it is my experience that the forgotten man or the canceled man will never disappoint you when you save him from drowning and that he will be the first to swim out into uncharted waters to rescue others when you ask him.

Any clown with social media followers and moral self-laudation can cancel someone. I believe in restoring opportunity and calling people to the best versions of themselves, not judging them at their worst. The only problematic people are the ones who don't seek to be better tomorrow.

No, I don't cancel. I uncancel. And I'm a better public servant because of it. No one is remembered for what he got, only for what he gave. So, let he who is without sin cast the first tweet. The rest of us are busy working together to make our union just a little bit more perfect, despite our imperfections.

CHAPTER FIFTEEN

AIR FORCE ONE: OF VICTORIES AND QUARANTINES

March 9, 2020
Air Force One. Departing Orlando Sanford International Airport.

"WRAP GAETZ IN CELLOPHANE!"

"Not necessary. I'll jump off with or without the parachute!" I shouted to the half-joking president just as the most famous airplane in the world was entering the clouds in ascent.

I was already being whisked past the conference room hosting my leather chair and personalized name card. Presidential Personnel Office Director and Trump buddy Johnny McEntee wasn't taking me to my seat. He was taking me to quarantine.

I wasn't even supposed to be on the plane. Earlier that day, I had attended a Trump 2020 fundraiser at the home of Bob and Diane Dello Russo. The Trump movement is so fun in part because it brings out such fun people. I would have loved to sip champagne with my best friends, all-around Orlando A-listers Chris and Rebekah Dorworth. They always draw a crowd of Florida's most interesting political minds and characters—but there was work to do.

Conducting the president's politics is joyous and engaging and busy. Supporters ranged from bundlers who had raised hundreds of thousands of dollars to important political figures representing the best of the Trump movement.

Chris Anderson served our nation in uniform in Afghanistan. He's never shaken the call to public service, having protected our communities as a law enforcement officer, and is now trusted as Seminole County's first-ever African American supervisor of elections. He and his wife, Ebony, a Democrat, weren't political for most of their lives but now represent how inspiring the bold leadership of President Trump can be to a wide cross-section of patriots.

Trump has the strongest work ethic of any man I've ever met— and he respects those on his team willing to put in the hours and the handshakes like he does. I took hundreds of pictures and gave at least as many hugs. In the Sunshine State, I've been on quite the political winning streak. I was a top ally of the president and of Governor Ron DeSantis, having worked like the devil to get both elected, at times against strong odds and stronger money. The record would suggest that in Florida, I'm a good friend to have. Even the state's top Democrat, Agriculture Commissioner Nikki Fried, is a close pal. In the words of FloridaPolitics.com's Peter Schorsch following the 2018 election cycle, the Florida political world was "Gaetz's Apalachicola oyster."

AT THE DELLO RUSSO HOME, A QUESTION WAS PUT TO THE PRESIDENT.

"We haven't gotten the housing money, Mr. President. Our people cannot rebuild if they have nowhere to live," said Cody

Khan, an immigrant hotelier revered in Panama City, where Hurricane Michael had carved a path of devastation. "Can you help us get what Congress appropriated?"

"Does your fine congressman know about this?" The president asked Cody the question, but looked directly at me for a response.

"Yes, sir, we need to get HUD to publish the rules sooner for Florida to program the money. Governor DeSantis is ready. We could use some help," I said.

"We will fix this on the plane. I will not tolerate delay. Construction delays hurt everything else. Matt, we will fix this. We will call whoever we need."

"Mr. President, I wasn't planning on joining…"

President Trump has a way of tilting his head down while he is seated and looking up at you. It's all in the steeliness of the eyes. He stopped me mid-sentence without uttering a word.

"Yes, sir. We will fix it on the plane." I had planned to drive to Tallahassee for other meetings. Those would have to wait.

I will forever be grateful that Rebekah returned my rental car and, in doing so, played a critical role in getting millions of dollars delivered to hurricane-ravaged communities in Northwest Florida.

The small Air Force One office where Johnny later led me during takeoff was close to the press cabin. Earlier, Peter Baker of the *New York Times* had tried to coax me back to his area for an interview. I doubt he would want one from a COVID-uncertain surrogate, though! For his was the last text I got before my chief of staff gave me the startling news during takeoff: someone who was positive for coronavirus and hospitalized had checked his phone for recent contacts. There I was in his photos, holding it, taking a selfie with the sweating, coughing admirer. People shed all their germs onto their phones. I'd later tell Amber Athey of the *American Spectator* that I might as well have licked his toilet seat!

Quarantine is no excuse for not working, though—especially when President Trump is giving the assignments. Throughout the flight, the president had Johnny pass notes back and forth to me regarding Florida's needs and our plan to meet them.

I ultimately tested negative. Tiger blood, maybe. No matter the reason, everyone I had hugged was relieved. And Florida got the money. Still, it wasn't the biggest cash haul that plane has delivered for my people.

May 8, 2019
Air Force One. Departing Joint Base Andrews for Panama City.

"So, your dad is a real big shot, huh?"

The president strutted into the conference room and tossed a Politico story from earlier that day onto the slick, polished table. It slid across into my lap. I knew what it said. My father, a highly respected former Florida State Senate President, had been quoted saying President Trump "owed the people of Northwest Florida an explanation" as to why he hadn't approved the maximum federal reimbursement to local communities for post-Hurricane debris removal. Sheesh. Thanks, Dad.

Hurricane Michael had slammed the state back in October 2018, not long before the gubernatorial election. In May 2019, Trump was flying to Florida for a political rally. Former OMB director Mick Mulvaney, now his acting chief of staff, had only arranged for 75 percent of the hurricane cleanup to be handled by the feds, but my state would save big bucks if the feds agreed to pick up 90 percent.

My father is my political hero and our service together in the Florida Legislature is among the most cherished times in my life. But on this, the day after my thirty-seventh birthday, he hadn't made my job easier. To be fair, I didn't always make his job easier with my aggressive views and style during our overlapping public service.

Fortunately, I had backup. Sen. Marco Rubio and Rep. Neal Dunn joined me in begging the president for a max federal cost share for Florida. Sen. Rick Scott (R-Puerto Rico) was also present.

After half an hour of debate and discussion, Trump had heard enough. He wanted to see the words and render a verdict. "Write down what you want me to say." He hadn't yet said he'd approve. He seemed to want to mull how it looked on paper and might sound if announced at the rally upon landing.

I raised the pen, acutely aware that what I wrote down could end up in a presidential speech and in federal policy—or doom Floridians hoping for that chunk of federal aid. This kind of magic moment only happens in Trump World. He understood this mattered a great deal—but he also wanted a quick, efficient decision. I knew he'd like big language, indicating that the additional federal funds would be an important boost to an important state with a lot of electoral votes.

He delivered my hastily prepared lines word for word. The crowd loved it. Florida needed it. Trump nailed it. Stagecraft is statecraft.

"That plane ride cost the taxpayers almost half a billion dollars!" Mick Mulvaney is a fiscal stickler and wasn't thrilled with my tactics. (It was $448 million, to be exact.) Mick's fiscal discipline is one of the reasons I admire him so much. But my people were legitimately in need. Mick knew the power of the crowd is, at times, stronger than the power of the purse strings.

Trump makes decisions by maximizing his inputs of information in nontraditional settings. A promise of different thinking was an organizing principle of his campaign. The contrast with the way his predecessor, President Obama, made decisions, is striking. David Plouffe's book about Obama, *The Audacity to Win*, depicted

Obama's team as wanting very few decision-makers at the top, thinking that makes the process easier and less bureaucratic.

Obama played things close to the vest. Trump, by contrast, constantly talks to people at the top levels of business, sports, entertainment, publishing, and Congress—even mere second-termers like me without a committee chairmanship—if he thinks we have valuable insight. Those conversations become an important early part of his decision-making process, as do arguments with his friends and close advisors.

This leads to the criticism that he reverses himself or thinks out loud. That's all part of his process. I'm sure glad it is.

May 30, 2020
Air Force One. Traveling to SpaceX launch
at Cape Canaveral, Florida. Presidential Office.

"THE RUSSIA INVESTIGATION WAS CORRUPT. IT WAS STARTED BY corrupt people, advanced before secret courts with fake evidence, and then repeated by media personalities and Democrats who now look like the liars and fools they are. No American should disproportionately shoulder the burden of the Mueller investigation. It should be relegated to history for what it was—a setup in search of crimes," I said, looking right at the president.

"Write that down. Write me three paragraphs. It can be longer. But say it just like that."

As I write, I'm certain that President Trump, in his willingness to fight, will also pardon Roger Stone—as well he should. I still talk to Roger on the phone. He's a bullshit artist and a dirty trickster, but no criminal. Our political operatives shouldn't end up in jail while some of the other team's still work at the Department of Justice and FBI.

"HAPPY BIRTHDAY, MY SWEET MOTHER!" HAVING THE AIR FORCE One operator connect us was a nice touch. I was about to watch Elon Musk bring humankind one step closer to multiplanetary species status. Here on Earth, though, my mother is the hero of my life. She no longer takes any steps. She has built businesses and wealth, has been married to my father for nearly four decades, and inspires everyone she meets, while treating people with empathy and love. My father got the highest vote margins, my sister Erin is the smartest and funniest, and I hold the highest office. But everyone in Northwest Florida knows my saint of a mother is the most popular Gaetz. She's also the strongest, and usually the prettiest.

My mother has been confined to a wheelchair for thirty-five years. A blood clot burst in her spinal column when she was pregnant with my brilliant sister. She was advised she could terminate her pregnancy and improve her own health odds. Many days she has pain she never mentions. She has no time for complaints. She is a woman always on the move. She won't allow anyone to push her—even sometimes up hills. She drives where she wants, maintaining the strength to sling her wheelchair over her body into the passenger seat like a gladiator. She won't let anyone else, including my father, drive her– but who could keep up with her anyway? She manages construction projects, participates in local animal welfare organizations, and serves as the CEO of the Gaetz Family.

In every campaign I've had, my mother's phone calls to potential voters have been noted by my opponents as my strongest weapon—and we've never lost an election. Watching her grind through call sheets during my first campaign for public office in 2010, my Catholic friend Mike Fischer observed, "If Jesus had run for state representative, I don't know if Mary would have made more voter contacts than Vicky Gaetz."

During my 2016 congressional campaign, a Republican primary opponent criticized me for self-designating as a "momma's boy." I learned to assemble a wheelchair when I was six years old. When my mother was ill, I slept in her hospital room against the rules to bring her comfort. I'm a serviceable cook today because I was her helper in the kitchen growing up. I'm a momma's boy with pride!

Calling my mother from Air Force One on her birthday was one of the best perks so far of my two terms in Congress. I'd love to tell you which birthday she was celebrating, but I'm still afraid of her.

CHAPTER SIXTEEN

A GREEN REAL DEAL

AMERICA IS NEITHER AN IDEA NOR A CONSTITUTION. IT IS OUR home—and we must keep our home clean and splendid from sea to shining sea. America will only be great if she is beautiful. Littering is a crime against nature. If we don't protect the small things, we certainly won't have the focus to protect what really matters. No, we cannot be "America First" if we allow her to be filthy. She deserves better. We cannot be a great nation strewn with trash. Our beauty is why so many come from far away to enjoy our shores, rivers, mountains, valleys, lakes, and beaches. While immigration romantics love citing that poem—"give us your poor...yearning to breathe free"—they rarely note that those huddled masses are not only breathing free but are breathing clean air. Can't say the same in Shanghai, Mexico City, Cairo, or even Rome.

Conservative, Inc.—bought off as always—would have you believe it's in your best interest for chemical plants to pollute our rivers, agribusiness to clog our estuaries with their runoff, and coal plants to darken our skies. This pollution even shows up in the human body. Atrazine and other industrial waste products turn us into fat, weak husks of humans. One of the few remaining advantages we have over China is that we love our country enough not to let her fall into squalid decay. We do need to get much better at it, though.

Washington bureaucrats fail us. They've been too dumb or too corrupt or too dishonest. Stewardship requires foresight and rewards planning that goes well beyond the quarterly reports, election cycles, or lobbying contract term lengths. The people engaged in the old conservative welfare scheme that converts corporate cash into D.C. sinecures seem to forget that we conserve nothing if we don't conserve our homes, our lands. We don't tolerate someone coming into our individual home, trashing the place, and then leaving. So why do we tolerate it in our cherished American environment?

Energy use correlates well with a higher standard of living, but we still have to make sure our world is livable. I reject the Leftist notion that environmental policy should be centered around conspicuous, pious, superficial, Instagrammable acts of individual sacrifice or virtue signaling. In caring for our planet, the Left prefers genteel hypocrisy. Lots of talk, no action. Green New Deal, but no compromise or execution. In other words, the exact opposite of the can-do American spirit.

My Catholic friends often talk about subsidiarity, an organizing principle that says matters ought to be handled by the smallest, lowest, or least centralized competent authority. The emphasis here is on competence. It sounds a lot like federalism. Few of our governmental institutions are at all effective, especially at the federal level. The Catholics start where Aristotle did—with the family, still the strongest institution in American society despite weird efforts to redefine it. Fathers must teach sons reverence for Creation and teach their sons to be gentlemen: gentle and careful with the natural world.

To be out in nature is to love it and to be awestruck by it. We're hardwired for it. We're grateful for the careful attention of those before us who had the wisdom to leave us space for the national parks, which continue to inspire generations of Americans. You never forget the first time you see a buffalo or a bald eagle in the wild. I wouldn't be the first American political populist to champion the greatness of America's wild spaces. That would be the great Theodore Rex, Teddy Roosevelt. Maybe the natural successor to a Bull Moose is a Florida Man.

From nature, we learn that there are duties that come with being our planet's apex predator. We have been entrusted by our station to care for all those below us, in much the same way we care for the weak or the sick or the infirm. The hippies speak often of thinking globally and acting locally. Part of loving your neighbor as yourself is loving your neighborhood and protecting it. We have a neighborhood watch. Why not an environmental watch made up of passionate citizens? If each of us took care of a sector close to us, we'd make the world a better place, and more importantly, we'd have fun out of the house. Charity begins at home and so too does conservation.

Unfortunately, we outsource our awesome responsibility to the trial lawyers and bureaucrats who run the Environmental Protection Agency, a bureaucracy that neither protects nor gives the public much agency to solve the environmental problems in their communities. The current EPA should be abolished and entirely reimagined.

To solve a problem, you must first acknowledge its philosophical underpinnings and limitations. For example, one of the critiques of animal rights is that you can't teach the cat to respect the rights of the dog. I prefer the term "humane" behavior to "rights-respecting" behavior. Humans shouldn't treat animals poorly, not only because it's bad for the animals but because it's bad for humans, bad for our character. Our EPA, by contrast, is an antihuman bureaucracy. It must be abolished before it abolishes the environment itself. We are our best selves when we realize and care about what's real.

Climate change is real. I did not come to Congress to argue with thermometers, only windbags. There is a scientific consensus that the Earth is getting warmer. There is a moral consensus that we should do something about it. I want to avoid frivolous fights over obvious science, just as I want my neighbors fighting fewer frivolous wars. Serious people take on serious challenges. Climate change requires our attention and our best minds. Assemble the nerds and unleash them. Every one of us walks around with more computing power than we used to land on the moon. What if we brought it to bear building probes, trackers, and sensors to make sure our environments were healthy? We could use GPS to help us navigate to a cleaner, better future.

Our environment is constantly spitting out data. We should analyze it for the public good. From our natural world, our nerds should take nothing but data and leave nothing but the lightest of footprints.

What climate change doesn't demand is a socialist takeover. Being smarter for our land and people doesn't require surrender to AOC's Green New Deal socialist Woketopia. I'll prove it.

Earlier this year, the secretary of the air force, the secretary of the army, and the chiefs of staff of both the army and the air force testified before the House Armed Services Committee that in real time, climate change is impacting the strategic decisions that our military makes regarding weapons testing, basing decisions, the global movement of people, and high-stakes territorial claims made by our geostrategic adversaries in the Arctic.

Keep in mind, this dire message is coming not from a smelly vegan drum circle banged out on a shit-stained sidewalk in San

Francisco or the nutty editorial staff of *Mother Jones* magazine. This warning is coming directly from the top brass of the United States military—the most lethal fighting force this world has known. Climate change is directly relevant to our national security, and it is relevant to our nation's border security, too. If you think the situation at the border is wild now, imagine a not-too-distant future of millions of climate refugees putting additional pressure on our nation's sovereignty—creating a global staging ground for terrorists and traffickers alike. Will we have the will to stop them? Or will we be among them? A failed environment could well be a precursor for a failed state. It usually is.

The question of how we treat our environment is directly related to how we treat our people. It might come as a surprise to many, yet makes perfect sense, that many of the most prominent environmental organizations in the United States originally supported an immigration position similar to that of President Trump's. Indeed, some of the most intense environmentalists were also the most serious immigration restrictionists. They knew that unchecked immigration and open borders would put unsustainable pressure on the nation's environment—our precious treasure. To secure our environment is to preserve our liberty. That which is ours, we will defend, this we know. But how? National security is border security is environmental security. Republicans should care about securing all three.

Republicans who ignore or dismiss climate change are therefore not only defying scientific consensus but sacrificing their real commitments and duties to preserve our union and its way of life.

Climate change is a real problem. Real problems require realistic solutions, not fantasy wish lists, and that is where the Democrats have failed miserably.

At present, the best-known Democrat proposal to tackle climate change is AOC's Green New Deal. It's not a viable action plan; it is a to-do list for things she and her colleagues want the government to control.

Say goodbye to cars, cows, airplanes, and buildings, and hello to $93 trillion in new spending. If you like your hamburger, you can't keep your hamburger.

Of course, the Green New Deal was never intended to be a serious proposal. Even its own sponsors ultimately refused to vote for it. It does, however, embody the regulatory impulse that is typical of Democrat approaches to all such problems. They seek to control; we seek to liberate. Free-thinking innovators will solve this problem faster than a constrained citizenry ever could.

When they are not calling for a major sector of the economy to be regulated into extinction, the Democrats are lecturing the American middle class about having too many children or, increasingly, telling us to eat insects for the good of the planet! You first, Alexandria! The regulatory approach favored by Democrats is not only unimaginative and unrealistic, but it is also counterproductive. Throwing more regulations at the problem simply ensures that we will outsource pollution-causing jobs overseas, to countries like China and India with substantially worse environmental protections than our own. I'm just not woke enough to export my pollution rather than solving it like a real American should.

In other words, Democrats' plans would not only destroy America's economy, they would fail to reduce global emissions. The Green New Deal would probably increase global emissions since polluting industries would immediately outsource all their operations to other nations. If anything, we should institute a carbon tax on China, not America. Or are we really going to pretend that the greatest polluters in the world are in the West?

Ten of the world's rivers account for 90 percent of ocean plastics. Seven of them are in Asia.

Power-hungry politicians and special interests in the United States will surely benefit from the displacement of our businesses overseas, but the American economy and the environment would suffer. Which, come to think of it, is precisely the point.

The notion of fighting climate change by destroying our economy is so absurd and counterproductive that it is sometimes unclear whether these policies are written by naïve but well-meaning children or by Chinese lobbyists themselves! Who can tell?

Instead of leaning on more regulation to address climate change, my Green *Real* Deal draws upon a precious natural resource that exists in happy abundance: the innovative spirit of the American people.

It might come as a surprise to some, but the president has already laid the foundations of an effective approach to climate change in his serious approach to China, not only on trade but on combating intellectual property theft. For decades, special interests and the establishment in charge sat back idly while jobs, livelihoods, and entire industries were stolen by China.

Apart from the tragic devastation these decisions wrought on so many American communities, the less-known tragedy is the devastating impact these de facto pro-China policies have had on the environment. Multinational industries—some polluting—outsourced to countries with no emissions standards, and the environment paid the price. The more we outsource, the less we can observe, and that's by design too.

Air knows no borders. Meanwhile, our one-sided trade relationship with China built up China's economy and increased global pollution—both at the expense of America's working people and industrial base. The garbage islands and the toxic clouds were made in China, too.

What's worse is that China's systematic plunder of American intellectual property weakened entrepreneurial incentives to innovate—including those innovations directly necessary to solve our climate change crisis.

America's solar technology once led the world. Not so anymore. China stole this intellectual property, replicated our products, and undercut the American solar industry. They had decided that our know-how was essential to their state interests, so they stole it. Oh, China.

Trump's tough approach to China's abusive trade practices rolls back our previous policy of subsidizing Chinese pollution while screwing American workers.

Additionally, the president's tough approach to China's IP theft builds the healthy ecosystem of American innovation necessary for lasting clean energy solutions. It isn't just China that has been holding us back from realistic solutions to climate change. As is so often the case, we are our own worst enemy.

We have no excuse for ignoring our electric grid. We can and must upgrade and modernize it. The American Society of Civil Engineers graded our grid D+. Today's grid can't even handle our existing portfolio of renewable energies, much less the expanded use our future requires. The National Renewable Energy Laboratory says today's renewable energy technology coupled with an updated grid could result in renewable energy meeting 80 percent of America's energy needs by 2050. If we can give oil companies tax write-offs for the costs associated with the pollution they cause, we can do more to encourage investment in the electric grid used by virtually every American.

"Net metering" technology allows property owners, shopping centers, hospitals, and schools among others to sell the energy they create back to our grid. In so doing, these new energy innovators create incentives for corporations to maximize domestic renewable energy production while allowing homeowners to lower or eliminate energy costs by embracing renewable energy. Energy entrepreneurs tinkering in garages and spare bedrooms—what is more American than that?

The Green Real Deal realizes that our electric grid ought to be a platform, not a bottleneck, to clean energy innovation and supremacy. We could also harness the 640 million acres of federally owned land. Why not extract more renewable energy from this repository and allow the bounties of our beautiful land to contribute to their own continued preservation? Reps. Paul Gosar and Raúl Grijalva have suggested as much, and it is a bipartisan no-brainer.

I've often described the Green Real Deal as a love letter to the American innovator. And I am proud to say that the innovative approach favored by the Green Real Deal would drastically reduce one of the most environmentally unfriendly materials known to man—RED TAPE.

Today's cheapest, cleanest energy is hydropower. A pro-hydro agenda should cut through the red tape, reducing costs for consumers along with carbon emissions. No longer should local concerns override national interest. The hydropower belongs to all of us.

The Green Real Deal would reduce the constraints on zero-emissions nuclear innovation, particularly where it can replace dirty coal. Currently, the Nuclear Regulatory Commission favors big, expensive light-water reactors that cost billions of dollars. Instead, the NRC ought to consider smaller, reliable modular reactors that can be built at a fraction of the cost, which would expand the availability of nuclear power to disadvantaged rural communities while using spent nuclear rods.

Modular nuclear power would also be invaluable to our military bases. By taking bases off the grid, the electric grid would become a less attractive target to hackers. Why can't we power San Diego or Honolulu with the nuclear reactors of the docked fleet?

Nuclear energy is clean, effective, and safe. Chernobyl is often cited as a reason to fear nuclear. To be fair, I wouldn't trust a toothbrush made in Russia in the early '80s, much less a nuclear plant. The technology has gotten better and better, though—and its absence from AOC's Green New Deal is as conspicuous as it is curious. In France, they've built massive nuclear reactors because their socialists correctly found them essential.

President Trump made history by addressing the needs of the forgotten man in rural America—and it is up to us to build on this achievement, to democratize nuclear use in our rural communities, and to ensure American companies capture the global modular nuclear market.

The ideas I put forth in the Green Real Deal are but the beginning of something interesting, but they are an important and necessary step toward an innovative, realistic solution to the real problem of climate change.

As with so many of the most important challenges we face, the stale political dogmas and divisions of the past do not help us see, much less solve, climate change. Young people of all ideological persuasions understand the importance of getting it right on climate change because their futures are at stake.

Protecting our environment is not an issue of Left versus Right—it is an issue of clean versus dirty, healthy versus sick, the beautiful against the ugly.

It is conservative in that most essential, nonpartisan sense— the sense of conserving the resources and splendor of our natural world. It is time to free the creative genius of this country to protect our natural treasures, and in so doing secure America's greatness, prosperity, and beauty for generations yet to come.

America is not just an idea. It is our skies, our oceans, our forests, and our home. Most of all, it is ours. And ours to lose.

ACKNOWLEDGMENTS

FIRSTLY, I WANT TO ACKNOWLEDGE MY CONSTITUENTS IN Northwest Florida. Thank you for placing your faith in me, for sending me to Washington to fight for you. In all I do, I put America, Florida, and our community above all else.

To President Donald J. Trump and First Lady Melania Trump—Washington wouldn't be the same without you. I can't fathom being in Congress under any other president. I couldn't ask for better leaders, allies, and friends.

To my parents, Don and Vicky—I wouldn't be the Firebrand I am today without your unconditional love, support, drive, and occasional patience. Thank you for the sacrifices you have made to give me a cherished life and every opportunity to make a difference. My sister, Erin, who has always been there for me no matter what—our blood runs thick. My son, Nestor—you bring me life's best moments; you have unlimited potential and I know you will go far. We are all behind you!

To my great friends—Donald Trump Jr, Kimberly Guilfoyle, Tiffany Trump, Michael Boulos, Ron and Casey DeSantis, Chris and Rebekah Dorworth, Jason Pirozzolo and Savara Hastings, Mike Fischer, Brianna Garcia, Charles Johnson, Suzanne Harris,

Larry Keefe, Andy Biggs, Jim Jordan, Mark Meadows, Thomas Massie, Nick Teman, James Parker, Harry and Allison Clayton, Tristan Tyler, Todd Purdy, the Bear family, Collier Merrill, Jay Odom, Joe Farrell, May Mendez, Kip Talley, Neal and Leah Dunn, Brian Ballard, Samantha Sullivan, Dawn McArdle, Jim Rimes, Ryan Smith, Rich Heffley, Charlie Kirk, and the many others I am forgetting as I rush this book to print. Life is more exciting with each and every one of you in it!

To Sergio Gor, whose energy was the spark for Project Firebrand. Thanks for always being there, much more to come.

To those who take a chance on me on a daily basis in the media—Sean Hannity, Mark Levin, Tucker Carlson, Jeanine Pirro, Laura Ingraham, Mike Huckabee, Chris Cuomo, Martha MacCallum, Steve Hilton, Lou Dobbs, Jesse Watters, and Hallie Jackson. Thank you for allowing me to speak up and defend America.

Thanks to my publishing team including Adam Bellow at Post Hill Press and his entire team, and to Todd Seavey who assisted from the conception of the project.

Finally, to my amazing congressional team led by Jillian Lane-Wyant—we work harder than anyone else. We demand excellence. We are in the thick of things on a daily basis and we wouldn't have it any other way. We have won many battles, and we will continue to do so. Thank you for believing in our mission.